A HISTORY OF
CHALFONT ST. PETER
&
GERRARDS CROSS
with
THE HISTORY OF BULSTRODE

Part of the 1822 edition 1 inch to 1 mile Ordnance Survey map, showing Bulstrode, Gerrards Cross and the Chalfonts.

A HISTORY OF
CHALFONT ST. PETER
&
GERRARDS CROSS

G.C. Edmonds MA

with

THE HISTORY OF BULSTRODE

A.M. Baker PhD, FSA

A History of Chalfont St. Peter and Gerrards Cross copyright © 1964, 1968
by Geoffrey Edmonds
The History of Bulstrode copyright © 2003 by Audrey Baker
Other material copyright © 2003 by Colin Smythe Limited

This double volume first published in Great Britain in 2003
by Colin Smythe Limited, Gerrards Cross, Buckinghamshire SL9 8XA

British Library Cataloguing-in-Publication Data

A catalogue record for this book
is available from the British Library

ISBN 0-86140-319-3

Produced in Great Britain
Typeset by PageSet Ltd and printed and bound by
T.J. International Ltd, Padstow, Cornwall

CONTENTS

Illustrations

Preface

This volume contains two works both of which are valuable to everyone interested in the history of the locality. The first, the late Geoffrey Edmonds' *A History of Chalfont St Peter and Gerrards Cross*, was published in 1964, followed by an enlarged version published by this company in 1968. That edition is reprinted here without revision, apart from the removal of the final section 'What Next'. According to the 2001 Census the population figures are now in the region of 7,340 for the parish of Gerrards Cross (which comprises 2½ wards, on which the census is based, hence the approximation) and about 13,000, for Chalfont St Peter. Audrey Baker's *The History of Bulstrode* is here published for the first time.

The Rev. Geoffrey Edmunds (1902–1975) served as Congregational Minister in Gerrards Cross from 1950 until his retirement in 1972, while Dr Audrey Baker was born before the first World War just before her parents moved to Latchmoor House (later renamed Walpole House).

To these works have been added over 100 illustrations — photographs, paintings and maps — relating to the two villages and to Bulstrode. We have aimed to publish pictures of those places and buildings that no longer exist or have been considerably modified since the pictures were taken or painted, rather than pictures of buildings as they exist at present.

In Gerrards Cross, the infill of the cutting between the bridges carrying Packhorse Road and Marsham Lane across the railway, and the building of the Tesco store on the newly created land (against the wishes of the vast majority of the local population) will inevitably impact and transform the centre of the village for the worse if only from the considerably greater volume of traffic that will result: the 'village' atmosphere will soon be gone. Already we have lost almost all the old family businesses: Bonsey's the butcher in Station Road, for example, was one such business that went back 300 years in the area; names familiar to me when this company moved to Gerrards Cross thirty-six years ago – Bott's, the County Garage, Percivalls, Poppies, Roff's, Sturley's, Worboys, to name but a few – have gone. Even Lovells, who built so much of Gerrards Cross, has moved elsewhere, and having a 'superstore' in the heart of the village will wipe out more.

It is a depressing thought that, on looking through *Binder's Directory of Gerrards Cross & Chalfont St Peter* for 1940, apart from the banks, and companies such as W.H.Smith, Boots, and the Ethorpe Hotel, only two names of local businesses that were in

Packhorse Road then are to be found there now: Aldridge's, the greengrocers, and Frosts, the estate agents. The rest exist only in memory.

August 2003   Colin Smythe

Acknowledgements

The publishers wish to thank the following organisations and individuals for their help in providing the illustrations in this book, on the pages as indicated.

John Andrews: 48b, 49a, 51b, 56b; Trustees of the British Museum: 143; Buckinghamshire Archaeological Society: iii; The Buckinghamshire County Museum and Centre for Buckinghamshire Studies collections: 17b, 18b, 19b, 21a, 22a, 23a, 50a, 54b, 55a, 56a, 57a, 57b, 83a, 83b, 156a, 156b, 158a, 158b, 159, 160; L.Chalenor: 26; J.Gates: 54a; The Gerrards Cross and Chalfont St Peter History Society: 16b, 17a, 18a, 19a, 20a, 20b, 21b, 22b, 23b, 24b, 25a, 25b, 49b, 50b, 52a, 52b, 53b, 55b, 115, 126; Gerrards Cross Memorial Centre: 53a; Ruth Hayden, for permission to reproduce the reconstruction of Mrs Delany's court dress and Mrs Delany's drawing of trees at Bulstrode, from her work, *Mrs Delany; her Life and her Flowers* (London: Colonnade/British Museum Publications, 1980); Leicestershire Museums, Arts and Records Service, for all the pictures from the Newton Collection of the Great Central and Great Western Railways' joint construction of the railway through Gerrards Cross prior to its opening in 1906: 79–82; Clive Lloyd: 59; Susan Morris for her good offices in obtaining for us the permission of the present owner to use the picture of Chalfont House by J.M.W.Turner reproduced on the front cover and 25b; The National Portrait Gallery, London: 131, 134, 145; Simmons Aerofilms: 15, 48a; and to WEC International for the use of the aerial photograph of Bulstrode on 88 and the back cover of this work.

Audrey Baker's thanks go 'to my cousin Paul Winby and his friend who helped me with the heraldry and the interpretation of the inscriptions on the brasses in Upton Church; to Mr William Lack who gave me much help and allowed me to reproduce plates from his book; to my friends, the late Anna Hulbert, and Mrs Barbara Lyddiatt for their photography; to Mr John Harris for allowing me to reproduce illustrations from his article on Bulstrode, and for information and plans he sent me of the interior of the house; to Ruth Hayden; to Mrs Gulard of the Bucks Archaeological Society; to Lady Phyllida Gordon Duff for information about the Ramsden family, to Mrs Penny Walker for typing and preliminary editing of the chapters, to Nigel Austin for helping me to tidy up the book, and to my publisher Colin Smythe, particularly for allowing me to reproduce rather more pictures than I expected I'd be allowed'.

A HISTORY OF CHALFONT ST. PETER & GERRARDS CROSS

G.C. Edmonds

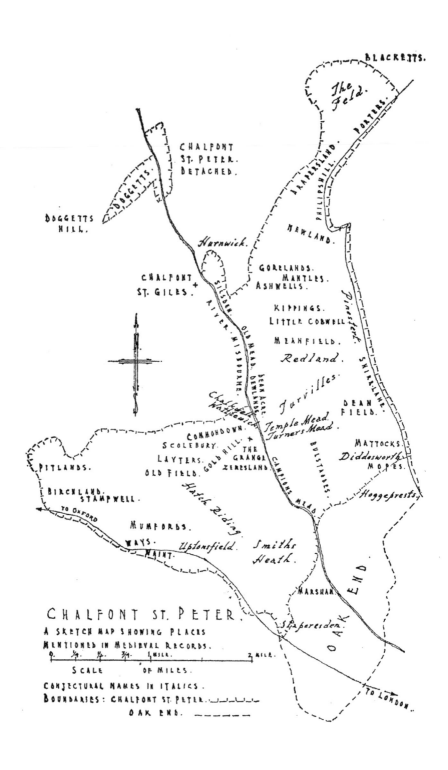

BLACKETTS.

The Field.

CHALFONT
ST. PETER.
DETACHED.

DOGGETTS.

DOGGETTS
HILL.

Harnwick.

CHALFONT
ST. GILES.

GORELANDS.
MANTLES.
ASHWELLS.

KIPPINGS.
LITTLE COBWELL

MEANFIELD.

Redland.

Jurvilles.

DEAN
FIELD.

Temple Mead.
Turners Mead.

MATTOCKS.
Diddesworth
MORES.

COMMONDOWN.
SCOLEBURY.
LAYTERS.
OLD FIELD.

THE
GRANGE
ZEBESLAND.

PITLANDS.

BIRCHLAND.
STAMPWELL.

Hatch Riding.

Hoggeprests.

TO OXFORD

MUMFORDS.

WAYS.
MAINT.

Uptonsfield.

Smiths
Heath.

MARSHAN.

CHALFONT ST. PETER.

A SKETCH MAP SHOWING PLACES
MENTIONED IN MEDIEVAL RECORDS.

0   ¼   ½   ¾   1 MILE.   2 MILE.

SCALE   OF MILES.

CONJECTURAL NAMES IN ITALICS.

BOUNDARIES: CHALFONT ST. PETER.

OAK END.

OAK END.

Shaperesden.

TO LONDON.

Forewords

This little book, the work of an amateur, owes much to the knowledge and encouragement of many friends. In particular, I wish to express my indebtedness to Mrs E.M. Elvey and her article on 'The Abbot of Missenden's Estates in Chalfont St. Peter', and to her and the Buckinghamshire Archaeological Society for permission to reproduce her map; to the President (E. Clive Rouse Esq., F.S.A.) and the Secretary (Dr Audrey Baker) of the Chalfont St. Peter and Gerrards Cross History Society; and to Mr and Mrs John Bennell. I hope that some of the fruits of Mr Bennell's careful studies will soon be published. Mr Eric Davis and Mr Veazey, of the County Record Office, have been unfailingly helpful.

I am especially grateful to Mrs Margaret Noble for typing the manuscript; to Mr Richard Harman, of the Blandford Press, for his kind interest in its publication, and to my wife for reading and correcting the manuscript and proofs.

There is much yet to be discovered about the history of these villages. Those who wish to pursue further any aspect of it are recommended to avail themselves of the help of the County Museum and County Record Office at Aylesbury, and of the local History Society, whose secretary, Miss Baker, lives at Carey House, Orchehill Avenue, Gerrards Cross.

G.C.E.
1964

The welcome demand for a second edition has given me the opportunity to correct some errors, insert some additional material, and add some notes and references.

The notes will make plain my indebtedness to some other friends besides those mentioned above, but I must also add here my thanks to the sympathetic publishers of this edition, Colin Smythe Limited.

1968

Since the last edition of this work there has been steady change in Gerrards Cross, and to a lesser extent in Chalfont St Peter.

There has been a lot of development in the centre of Gerrards Cross. For instance the Congregational (now United Reformed) Church where my father was minister has been pulled down and replaced by a modern church over a row of shops. In 1968 we still used to refer to Gerrards Cross as "the Village" but anyone seeing the substantial modern buildings in Station Road would hardly refer to the place in such rustic terms.

There has been much residential development too, particularly new houses put up in the large gardens. Despite the higher density of dwellings Gerrards Cross was recently pronounced to be the most expensive place for residential property in the Country. That reflects the fact that it is still a very pleasant place to live.

Gerrards Cross and Chalfont St Peter are now located near the intersection of two motorways, with the M25 running only about a mile east of the centre of Gerrards Cross and the M40 not more than a mile to the south.

The railway is now part of the Chiltern Line which has faster smarter trains, more numerous too, out of the rush hour, with an hourly train service to Birmingham.

There has been a proposal to cover over the railway cutting running through the centre of Gerrards Cross with a Tesco Store carpark, though this seems to be in abeyance at the moment. There is also a plan to develop the railway as a new super-route for Rail freight with huge trains running from the Channel Tunnel to Liverpool rushing through every quarter of an hour, which is revived every now and again. It will be interesting to see whether these or any other major projects are implemented in the next thirty years or so.

GRAHAM EDMONDS
June 2002

Introduction

This book attempts to set out something of the story of Chalfont St. Peter and Gerrards Cross. Of course, history cannot really be fenced off so neatly as this; these two villages have always had, as they have now, many links with the towns and villages around them. Amersham ('Agmondesham', as it used to be) was our market town; many families had members and lands in both Chalfont St. Peter and Chalfont St. Giles; Gerrards Cross had many associations with Denham, Iver ('Evre'), Fulmer ('Fugelmere') and Hedgerley ('Huggeley' or 'Hegeley'). But for reasons of time and space, it seemed best to resist temptations to wander into neighbouring parishes. Fortunately there are, besides Country Histories and several books on 'The Chilterns' and 'The Penn Country', published histories of Denham, Iver, and Fulmer, and of Chalfont St. Giles Church, for those who wish to go further.[1]

But first let us see what the parishes of Chalfont St. Peter and Gerrards Cross *are*.

Chalfont St. Peter and Gerrards Cross

Chalfont St. Peter is an ancient village, Gerrards Cross a new-comer. The ecclesiastical parish of Gerrards Cross was formed in 1859, but it did not become a civil parish until 1895. It was formed by taking pieces out of five parishes – Chalfont St. Peter, Iver, Fulmer, Upton and Langley Marish.[1] There is still a stone by the Oxford Road (not far from St. James's Church) which marks the spot where the parishes of Chalfont St. Peter and Fulmer met. Chalfont St. Peter is a large parish still; but for most of its life it extended from a point beyond Chorley Wood to a little south of the Oxford Road. 'Gerrards Cross Common' was 'Chalfont Heath', and adjoined 'Fulmer Heath'.[2]

Early Days

From Camp Road, Gerrards Cross, a path leads to an open space bought by the Parish council for the benefit of the public. This quiet and pleasant field fringed with trees, and surrounded by high banks and ditches, is the Bulstrode Camp, the largest fortified earthwork in the country. It appears not to have been a permanent home but a place of refuge. On the sides of the valleys round about, many flint implements have been found; and we may imagine the Iron Age inhabitants of this part of Bucks. Laboriously building these defences with such primitive tools, and then, when enemy tribes approached, hastily gathering their families and their cattle into this place of refuge. 'Bulstrode' first appears as 'Burstrod' (with a short 'u') and the place-name authorities tells us that it means 'the marsh belonging to the fort'.[3]

There are few streams on this side of the chilterns, and many dry valleys. As local gardeners know well, the soil is stony, and water quickly drains away. Mr J.F. Head, in his valuable book, *Early Man in South Buckinghamshire* shows how sparse are the signs of settlements in prehistoric times: and even of Roman occupation there is little evidence, apart from a few coins, and remains of Roman pottery kilns at Fulmer and Hedgerley. There are pockets of clay and brick-earth hereabouts which have encouraged the manufacture of bricks, tiles and pottery all through the centuries.

By one of the few streams, Chalfont grew up. The Misbourne River is not a very large river, and from time to time it disappears altogether; but it is still a charming stream when it sparkles in the sunlight. It flows through a pleasant valley from Missenden to

Denham, and it has watered our beasts and turned our mills through many generations.

The name 'Chalfont', the authorities tell us, comes from 'Ceadeles Funta' or 'Ceadel's spring', 'Ceadel' being a personal name (as in 'Chaddleworth', Berks.). Mr Head writes: 'The features that repelled settlement and cultivation in early Saxon times were, as might be expected, attractive to outlaws, political exiles, or other refugees. Romano-Britons in rebellion, or unable to adjust themselves to changed conditions, may well have found this hilly no-man's land a welcome retreat. And in this connection it will be recalled that the Place-Name Society, in their Bucks. volume, tell us that each part of the name Chalfont – Ceadeles funta – is of British origin.'

Domesday and After

When William the Conqueror sent out his commissioners in 1086 to make a detailed survey of his realm, they found that 'Chalfont' had already been split into two parts (later known as 'St. Giles' and 'St. Peter'). In both there were small organised communities: and the irregular boundary between them shows that outlying settlements were already in existence when, in Saxon times, the boundary was determined. It seems probable that that half-mile of the Misbourne Valley round about 'Oak End' had also originally been part of Chalfont, but had early been taken by a free tenant into the parish of Iver.

No doubt the village of Chalfont St. Peter first grew up by the Misbourne and around Gold Hill Common; but the figures given in the Domesday Survey suggest that already by that time new clearings in the forests were being made and new fields put under the plough in the higher lands. Two roads skirted the parish – Shire Lane, an ancient track which for several miles still forms the boundary between Buckinghamshire and Hertfordshire, and the medieval London to Oxford road, still more or less followed by the A40; and, as we shall see, scattered farms and hamlets sprung up near these two roads.

The village was one of the many which William granted to his doughty half-brother, Biship Odo, from whom it was held, feudal-fashion, by one of his knights, Roger d'Anquetil. Roger was the ancestor of the family of Turville, who held many lands in Bucks. and whose name is still recalled in 'Weston Turville'. In that tough but pious age, when many churches were built and many monasteries founded, one of the Turvilles built a church in our Chalfont, which was dedicated to St. Peter. In 1196 Richard de Turville gave it to the Augustinian Abbey of Missenden, which had

8

been founded 60 years earlier. In the same period a church was built in 'the other Chalfont' dedicated to St. Giles, and bestowed upon Bradwell Priory.[4]

In the same period, again, the Knights Templars, that famous Order, formed at the time of the Crusades, for the defences of Jerusalem and the protection of pilgrims, founded a House at Hedgerley, long afterwards known as Temple Bulstrode. The land appears to have been given to them by Henry de Pinkeni, who at that time held Fulmer manor, and before the end of the twelfth century it had been augmented by grants of land in neighbouring parishes. Richard de Turville gave them 130 acres in Chalfont St. Peter (on which was a water-mill) which came to be known as 'Turvilles land'.

A few years later land beside the Alderbourne with 'Prestwick' (the 'priests's dwelling') was given to Ankerwyke Priory, from which grew Alderbourne Manor.

In the early years of the next century, many lands in Chalfont St. Peter were given to Missenden Abbey, some by great landowners, some by lesser men, who often took them back at a rent. For example, about 1210, Robert de Braibrock, Sheriff of Bedfordshire and Buckinghamshire, granted to the Abbey land he had acquired from Richard de Turville: 'All the land which Thomas de Latier held in Chalfont, and all the land which Robert Kipping held, with Robert himself and his issue, and all the land of the assarts [clearings] in Chalfont which belonged to Richard de Turville.' Here we see afar off 'Newland' (near Shire Lane, the largest and possibly the oldest of the 'new lands' in Chalfont), Layters and Skippings farms, and probably some of the farms near the Oxford Road.

Thus in these years the Abbey was able to build up a 'manor' in Chalfont St. Peter, an estate whose tenants owed varying feudal duties and services to the Abbot. The process did not go unchallenged. In 1229 Henry II's Treasurer, Ranulf de Brito, obtained from the king 'the manor of Chalfont St. Peter'. He probably bought it as a speculation – without knowing or caring very much about the Abbot's rights – with a view to development. He obtained the right to hold an annual fair on July 28 and 29, and a market day every Wednesday. He also set to work with a high hand to bring the whole village under his control. His men invaded 'Mumfords', Ralph de Montfort's farm, took his corn, drove away his beasts, and finally imprisoned Ralph himself (the Abbot's free man). Geoffrey le Stamp had to suffer the loss of his fuel from Stampwell. The Templars' land in Chalfont was also attacked, and their goods distrained. But in 1231 Ranulf Brito was disgraced and banished; the Abbot promptly counter-attacked, and regained all the lands which Richard de Turville had given, together with some houses which Brito had built in the village. All that was left to Brito, when he returned, was 200 acres or so which he had acquired from another de Turville: this is the estate which later emerges as 'Brudenells Manor', centring on 'Chalfont Park'.[5]

In 1229, a vicarage was appointed in the church; and our first vicar was Walter of Aylesbury. Of the church lands which had been granted to the Abbey, the Abbot retained only two houses; the rest (together with Ranulf Brito's houses in the village) were held as a small manor by the vicar himself.

The Templars at Bulstrode

The Templars' House probably stood on or near the site of Moat Farm. (There used to be a lane leading east from that point called Temple Lane.) Little is heard of them, beyond the fact that Henry de Pinkeni (before 1200) had granted them the right to pasture 300 sheep on Fulmer Common; and an Assize case in 1276, when Brother John, the Preceptor, was accused of taking a bribe of half a mark from a certain robber to let him go free. But when, in 1308, the Order was suppressed in England, Edward III seized its very considerable property and goods; and the inventory made then gives an interesting glimpse of their life at Bulstrode. The simple house included a hall, with two tables and trestles, two sleeping tables, and a bell in the rafters; a well-furnished chapel; a kitchen; a cellar (with barrels); a bakehouse, and a workshop, with anvil and hammers. A chaplain, Edmund de Burnham, received for daily services $15\frac{1}{4}$d a week, plus an allowance of corn. A useful source of income was the water-mill on 'Turvilles land'. Though their stock was mixed, they evidently specialised in sheep: the inventory includes '100 sheep, 125 mother-sheep, seventy-five hoggetts, four rams and sixty lambs'. The wool was carted to London, and the stock-in-hand included 304 fleeces, fifty-six lamb-fleeces, thirty lamb-skins, and forty-four sheep skins. The staff included three carters, a mower, a cowkeeper, two shepherds, a swineherd, a ploughman; 16 women were paid for winnowing the corn.[6]

After the disappearance of the Templars, the manor of Temple Bulstrode passed through several hands, until in 1337 it was bestowed upon Bisham Priory (near Marlow) who held it for the next 200 years.

Oke

Of that detached portion of Iver which is variously called Ake, Oke, Noke and Oak End, we know little in these early years, except that it included a watermill and a tile works. The tile-works was probably near the site of 'Chalfont Lodge', which used to be Tilehouse Farm. In 1315 William atte Noke paid a rent of 3s 4d, three quarters of lime, 3,000 common tiles, and thirty ridge tiles. Tiles were supplied to Windsor Castle in 1353. Traces of the watermill can still be seen near 'Oak End'. It was acquired in the thirteenth century by a family named de Chaunceaux, and more than 300 years later was still called 'Chauceys Mill alias Noke Mill'.[7]

Under Missenden Abbey

For more than 350 years, Chalfont St. Peter was linked with Missenden Abbey. This story has been admirably told by Mrs E.M. Elvey in an article in *Records of Buckinghamshire* (vol. 17, pt. 2), based upon a study of the manor court rolls. You will see from her map (reproduced on page 2) of the fourteenth century manor, how many of the old names still persist.[8]

According to a rental of 1333, Matthew de la Vache (Chalfont St. Giles) was then the tenant of the 'the Feld' and Philips Hill, and John de Asschewelle had 'Ashwells'. At that time Geoffrey de Bulstrode held what we call 'Chalfont Park', and also those lands called 'Turvilles', which had formerly belonged to the Templars (concerning the ownership of which there was a long dispute).[9] John atte Grove ('Grove Park', Narcot Lane) had 'Diddesworth'; Thomas Mareschal, 'Molp' ('Mopes'); and Philip Durdent of Denham held 'Marsham' (which first appears as 'le Maysham' and later as 'Messam') and also a 'Boterfeld' holding ('Butterfield' is a recurring local name). Robert le Mountefort had 'Mumfords', and Sir Ralph de Wedon 'Birchlands' and 'Pitlands', near the Beaconsfield boundary.

'Old Mead', the long narrow strip between the Misbourne and the Amersham Road, formed the precious communal water-meadow. Common Downs, Skolebury, and Old Field were the great Common Fields in which each tenant had his strip, or strips, separated by 'balks' from his neighbour's land.

Soon Latchmoor Common Field ('le Hatch Ryding') was added; and there were other common fields on the other side of the valley, as the name 'Chalfont Common' still recalls.[10]

In the manor-court, held twice a year (sometimes more frequently), and disputes settled, some of the land was held by men important in the outside world, over whom the Abbot had little control. Some was held by free tenants, who were not slow to maintain their rights. There were, for example, Nicholas le Plomer and his nephew Nicholas, who in 1333 had Layters and Stampwell and other holdings along the Oxford Road (from one of which, that of Gerard de Chalfont, Gerrards Cross probably takes its name).

Young Nicholas went hunting and caught hares and partridges in the lord's warren. When he was admonished, his uncle produced a charter granted by an earlier abbot, giving them leave 'to hunt and fish in all the lands, woods and waters of the Lord Abbot which he has in the vill of Chalfont'. The Plomers, like their neighbour Robert de Montfort, declined to do homage in the Abbot's court, until the Abbot took the case before the King's Justices, who upheld his claim.

Even the villeins, the unfree tenants, though subject to many disabilities, had their rights protected by custom and upheld in the manor court. They were bound to do certain carefully defined services in the lord's fields, to keep their houses in good repair and their land in good heart. But they could sell their land if they wished and they could settle it upon their heirs.

A tenant's land might be in a compact block, together with a few strips in one of the common fields, like that of Richard Butterfield who held a house called Redland and 30 acres, with six strips in a common field call Denefield; or it might be scattered about in several common fields.

The village suffered, like others, from the Black Death in 1346; and here, as elsewhere, after that catastrophe, labour was in short supply and properties fell into decay. Before the end of the century, services owed to the Lord of the Manor were generally commuted into a money-rent. Thus, in 1401, John Boterfeld was admitted to a house and 30 acres 'to be held by him and his, according to the custom of the manor; rendering annually at the Feasts of the Annunciation of the Blessed Mary and of St. Michael 4s in equal installments and at Christmas 12½d, reaping the lord's corn for two days with food supplied by the lord, and for two days maintaining himself, carting the lord's corn for one day at his own expense and scything the lord's meadow for one day at his own expense, and haymaking for one day at his own expense, and ploughing the lord's land for two days at his own expense, or he must give the lord 14d. And he will hoe then the lord's land for one day at his own expense. And he shall do the lord's repairs to the extent of five wooden stakes, and then have breakfast from the lord. And on the Vigil of St. Thomas the Apostle he shall give one cock. And he shall make suit of court every three weeks and heriot* when it happens. And above this he gives the lord as a fine for entry upon the land 13s 4d. And he did fealty to the lord, and it is granted by the lord that the said John and his heirs may choose, either to hold the aforesaid lands and tenements in manner of form aforesaid, *or* to pay annually at the Annunciation of the Blessed Mary and of St. Michael 8s 9½d instead of the rent and works above mentioned.'

*Heriot, a fine due on the death of a tenant.

Fifteenth-century Abbots, struggling to keep things going, found themselves up against two powerful men in Chalfont. One of these you may meet in the church. There is a good brass there, of a man in plate-armour and a woman with horned headdress and veil, which commemorates 'William Whappelode, sometimes steward of the household of the most reverend Father in God, the most illustrious Lord Henry (Beaufort) Cardinal of England and Bishop of Winchester'. (Another brass commemorates his parents.) William Whappelode acquired the Vache manor at Chalfont St. Giles in 1411, and soon became the most powerful man in the district, representing Bucks. in Parliament, and holding other offices in the Country. He held many lands in Chalfont St. Peter and refused to pay rent for them. In his will of 1447 he expressed the wish to be buried 'in a chapel of the Church of St. Peter, before our Lady's altar, where my father and mother are buried'. He also charged his executors – 'as they will answer before the High Judge at the Day of Doom' – to make provision for prayers to be offered for the souls of himself and his wife. This they did by endowing a Chantry in the Church of St. Peter, with rents amounting to £7 per annum from Mumfords and other properties, from which the stipend of a chantry priest was paid.[11]

One of his executors was his friend and neighbour, Edmund Brudenell, of Raans manor in Amersham and 'Brudenells' manor in Chalfont St. Peter. This Edmund's grandson, another Edmund, proved himself an aggressive landlord, buying up all he could, and bullying the Abbot's tenants. For a long time past there had been a trend towards turning over arable land to sheep farming, which was more profitable; and Edmund evidently decided to cash in on this. He bought the remainder of the lease of the Grange lands, and allowed the house to go to ruins. In one of the earlier attempts of the State to check enclosures (1517) it is recorded that Brudenell had enclosed Layters and Butterfields 'which time out of mind had been ploughed and sown' and also another farm called Hogpittes (near the site of Coldharbour Farm). In each case the house had been allowed to fall into decay, and altogether 22 persons had lost their livelihood and been 'driven away in misery'.[12]

Edmund did much to destroy the traditional way of life in the Abbot's manor, which was already crumbling, before, in 1538, Henry VIII decreed the dissolution of the monasteries. In that year Edmund Brudenell died, and his estates in Chalfont St. Peter passed to his daughter, the wife of Sir Robert Drury; and a new era in our history begins.

But before we enter the reign of the Drurys, let us first look at some old houses, take a walk to Horn Hill, and then return to meet some neighbours of the Drurys.

Old Houses Rediscovered

Reminders of those times still occasionally come to light. Hill Farm appeared to be a seventeenth-century house, with considerable later additions. But a thorough examination, in 1967, revealed that the core of the house was a fourteenth-century open hall, with timbers still blackened from the open fire in the centre. In the following century, the master, or his dame, wanting more spacious private accommodation, had added a wing of two full storeys; and late in the seventeenth century the old hall had been divided, and a floor inserted. The original hall had an open crack truss, rarely found in this region; and the many alterations and conditions had left in one building the whole story of roof construction.

An even more striking example of what may lie behind a nineteenth-century mask was discovered when houses opposite the church were demolished in 1966 to make room for redevelopment. One, which had been divided, was found to be a substantial fifteenth century timber-framed house, with open hall and wings, having crown post roof-trusses and a splendid stone fireplace.[12a]

The big house in 'Chalfont Park', long known as 'The Old House', was a house of great importance in the life of the village – perhaps the house in which Edmund Brudenell and Sir Robert Drury lived. During alterations there in 1966 a wall and doorway of a fifteenth or sixteenth-century house were discovered on the south side.

Horn Hill

There is a farm at West Hide (in the parish of Rickmansworth) called Linsters. This was once the centre of a small manor, which included most of the farms and houses of Horn Hill, and lands in Chalfont St. Peter. It was held in the fifteenth century by members of the Lynster family, but by 1520 had passed to the hospital of the Savoy. When, soon after this, the lands of the Savoy came to the Crown, King Edward VI, in 1553, 'considering and pondering upon the scandalous and wretched condition of the poor, sick and infirm men now lying begging in the public places and ways of the City of London to their no slight grievance and pain', gave to St. Thomas's Hospital the Manor of Linsters, West Hide. Horn Hill, one of the most ancient, remains one of the most charming portions of the parish of Chalfont St. Peter, but it has an intricate history of its own, as most of its houses stood in Hertfordshire.[13]

The Legend of Bulstrode

One of the most distinguished members of the family of Bulstrode

An Aerofilm view of Chalfont St Peter, viewed from above Austenwood Common, in 1934.

Above: the High Street, Chalfont St. Peter, viewed from the Market Place, c.1919, with a group of very interested children. Below: the rear of Barrack Yard, in which eighteen families lived, which ran down to the river, which often flooded the ground floors of the cottages. Demolished in 1938, it was the site of a coaching inn, The Crossed Keys [of St Peter], and its entrance was almost opposite the Library.

Above: Chalfont St Peter. The water-splash on the river Misbourne in front of the Greyhound Inn, c. 1900, before it was entirely covered over. Below: a view looking up Gold Hill, now Market Place, c. 1905.

Above: the Workhouse building. With its closure, it was converted into four cottages, then shops, and demolished in 1978. The Library now stands on its site. Below: Mrs Grieve, whose husband was a noted antiquarian, set up a herb preparation business at The Whins, growing most of the herbs herself. Apart from the activities described on the card, dried and drying herbs are to be seen hanging from the ceiling.

Weighing, washing & Grinding at Mrs Grieve's, The Whins, Chalfont St Peter.

Above: a view from in front of the Workhouse down the High Street towards the church. Below a watercolour of the same view, the inn at the left being the White Hart. Both pictures date from c.1900.

Brown's Smithy, one of Chalfont St Peter's old shoeing forges, at the bottom of Joiner's Lane, and below, a later photograph when the owners had moved into the carriage business, with the wall of Swan Farm to the right, viewed from roughly where the roundabout is today.

Above: a school photograph, c. 1900. The writing on the slate reads (despite the presence of a boy in the picture) 'Chalfont S. Peter Girls [Gro]up 3'. Below: the Water Hall Hotel on the Amersham Road, is now a private house.

Above: Hill Farm from the front gate. The land around the house had been sold and the house fell into disrepair before being demolished.
Below: Austenwood Common and Holly Tree Farm.

59257. GERRARDS CROSS. AUSTEN WOOD COMMON.

Above: a garden fete at The Grange (now the Holy Cross Convent), Chalfont St Peter, in 1934, with Mrs Leeming, the wife of the then owner, receiving a bouquet from a girl in a Dutch national costume. Below: the obelisk at the entrance of the Chalfont Colony, c. 1940. The top half collapsed in 1964 when struck by lightning and only the bottom part now stands.

(Above) 'Chalfont House [as Chalfont Park was then called] in Buckinghamshire, the Seat of Thomas Hibbert Esqr. Published as the Act directs June 1st 1793 by W. Angus' (the engraver), after a painting by Charles Tomkins, and another view (below), c.1820–30, the house much enlarged, including the addition of a clock tower published in 1812, it was 'engraved by [Thomas Lord] Busby for the European Magazine'. The Hibbert estate was broken up and sold in 1888.

Above: Watercolour of 'Chalfont House', by J.M.W. Turner c. 1810.
Below: Chalfont Park, at the time it was a hotel, in the late 1930s. Prior to
its acquisition by British Aluminium, it was for a time a training centre for
the National Provincial Bank.

The Misbourne River in flood. Later the local water authorities extracted so much water upstream that it was reduced to a trickle at the time the M25 Motorway was built, but with extraction cut back the river now flows again, to the extent that with heavy rainfall in 2000 the Greyhound Inn in Chalfont St. Peter was flooded and rendered uninhabitable. It was reopened in 2002.

was Sir Richard, who died in 1711, at the age of 101. In the following years a volume of his letters was published, and in the preface is this story:

'When William the Conqueror had subdued this Kingdom to his Obedience, he granted the Estate of the Shobbingtons, whose capital Seat, now likewise called Bulstrodes, was situated in the middle of a fine park by Gerrards Cross near Beaconsfield, and had been in their Family for several ages before, to a certain Norman lord who had come over to him: of which the Shobbington, who then enjoyed it, having notice, he resolved rather to die upon the Spot, than tamely to suffer himself to be turned out of Possession of that Inheritance, which had descended to him from his Ancestors. In this Resolution he armed his Servants and his Tenants, whose Number was very considerable. Upon which the Norman Lord, who had advice of it, obtained of the King a thousand of his Regular Troops, to help him take Possession of the Estate by Force, whereupon Shobbington applied himself to his Relations and Neighbours to assist him: and two ancient Families of the Hampdens and Penns took Arms, together with their Servants and Tenants, and came to his Relief. When they were all joined, they cast up Works, whose Remains appear to this Day, in the Place where the Park now is; and the Norman Lord, with his Forces, came and encaped before their Intrenchements. Now whether that they wanted Horses, or not is uncertain, but the Story goes, That having managed a parcel of Bulls, they mounted them and sallying out of their Intrenchments in the night, surprised the Normans in their Camp, killed many of them, and put the Rest to Flight. The King having Intelligence of it and not thinking it safe for him, while his Power was yet new and unsettled, to drive a daring and obstinate People to despair, sent a Herald to them: to know what they would have, and promised Shobbington a Safe Conduct, if he would come to court; which Shobbington accordingly did, riding thither upon a Bull. Being introduced into the royal Presence, the King asked him his Demands, and why he alone dared to resist, when the rest of the Kingdom had submitted to his Government, and owned him for their Sovereign? Shobbington answered, That he and his Ancestors had long been inhabitants of this Island, and had enjoyed that Estate for many years; that if the King would permit him to keep it, he would become his Subject, and be faithful to him, as he had been to his Predecessors. The King gave him his Royal Word, that he would, and immediately granted him the Free Enjoyment of his Estate. Upon which the Family was from hence called Shobbington, alias Bulstrode, but in Process of time the first Name was discontinued, and that of Bulstrode only has remained to them. The Truth of this Story is not only confirmed by long Traditions in the Family, but by several Memoirs which they have still remaining, and by the Ruins of the Works, that are to this Day seen in the Park of Bulstrodes, as well as by the Crest of their Arms, which is a Bull's Head Cabossed Gules.'

One wonders what lies behind this splendid story. Perhaps some legend of an heroic exploit: more certainly, some family connection with the village of Shabbington (near Thame). It may well be that there were Bulstrodes on that hill where 'Bulstrode' now is before the Conqueror came: for the name appears in these parts early in the twelfth century. There they long continued, a line of minor gentry, in their small manor which is generally called 'Hedgerley Bulstrode' to distinguish it from 'Temple Bulstrode'.

Hedgerley Bulstrode was until the nineteenth century in a curious detached portion of Upton: and the family owned other lands at Upton, Chalvey, and Horton.[14] Sir Richard Bulstrode, who died in 1503, was Keeper of the Wardrobe to Henry VI's Queen Margaret: Edward, his son, Squire of the Body to Henry VII and Henry VIII. Edward married three times: a brass in Upton Church represents him with wife No. 1 and four sons, and wife No. 2 with six sons and two daughters: a brass in Hedgerley Church commemorates his third wife and her ten children.[15]

Robert Drury served on various county commissions with George Bulstrode and his son Thomas. Thomas died in 1560, and his will is worth recalling. He describes himself as 'Thomas Bulstred of Hedgerley Bulstred in the Parish of Upton, esquire'. His confession of faith is stoutly Protestant (three Protestants had been burnt at the stake in Uxbridge three years earlier). He quotes, from the Genevan version, *Job* c. 19 vv. 25–27 ('I know that my Redeemer liveth . . .') and hopes that his bestowal of his goods may be accepted as 'fruit of faith': 'I do not suppose my merit be by good bestowing of them, but my merit is the faith of Jesus Christ only'. 'A godly sermon' is to be preached at his burial 'by some godly and well-learned man not under the degree of Master of Arts'; another, when the month is up: and another, when the year is up. He leaves to his son Francis his manor in Horton, his long-bow, the quiver of shafts and arrows, a corselet and a pike: and to his son Edward, all his books, his poll-axe, daggers, sword, and cross-bow, and a quiver of arrows and bolts. After other bequests to relatives, servants, and the poor, he leaves the residue to his wife Ann: 'She shall have my house at Hedgerley as I did use to occupy it, and my farm at Coltnet (Horton), to keep these houses in good repair, and not to let them, except to a son.'[16]

Thomas was succeeded by his son Edward. This Edward was the grandfather of the Sir Richard Bulstrode mentioned above, who became Ambassador at Brussels, and died at the age of 101. One of Edward's daughters married Sir James Whitelocke, and became the mother of Bulstrode Whitelocke, historian of the Commonwealth;

another, Cicely, a court beauty of wit and high character, was celebrated in verse both by Ben Jonson and by John Donne.[17]

But to return to the Drurys, and to the time of Henry VIII.

The Drurys

The Drurys were an East Anglian family.[18] Sir Robert, a barrister who was elected Speaker of the House of Commons in 1495, had two sons – William, who carried on the line at Hawsted in Suffolk, and Robert, who married Elizabeth Brudenell and settled in Chalfont, leasing lands from the last Abbot of Missenden. When Elizabeth's father died, Robert Drury came into possession of the manors of Brudenells and Hedgerley in his wife's right. In the same year (1538) he bought, for £412, the Temple Bulstrode manor. Two years later, after the dissolution of the monasteries, he acquired the Abbot's manor in Chalfont St. Peter, with pieces in Chalfont St. Giles and Iver. Soon afterwards he bought both Turvilles land and the Chantry lands. He was now monarch of almost all he surveyed, and for the first time all our manors (except Hedgerley Bulstrode) were brought together under one ownership.

He was evidently a capable man, and a just man: and Chalfont St. Peter benefited from his strong rule. A new life comes into the court-rolls. Some, at least, of those who had long ignored the Abbot were brought to heel. Houses were rebuilt, order restored in the common fields, encroachments checked, hedges and balks reinstated, ditches cleared, pigs ringed, and the village pound repaired. Old customs were summarized: strays are to be proclaimed in church and market place; poaching is punished, whether in woods, warren or stream, but a common net to catch coughs, crows and rooks is allowed as of old. Constables and ale-tasters are appointed. John Fox the baker is fined for selling bread without licence, and William Bocher the butcher, for overcharging.

Sir Robert Drury was three times Sheriff of Bucks. – he was knighted on the first occasion, in 1546 – a loyal supporter of King Henry VIII, who served on various county commissions. The parish register records the burial in 1577 of 'that venerable man, Robert Drury, knight, Lord of the Manor and Patron of this Church', and there is elsewhere a record of his tomb which stood in the chancel.[19] One of his sons, Sir William, was Marshal of Berwick and Lord Chief Justice of Ireland, in the time of Elizabeth I (there is a portrait of him in the National Portrait Gallery). Another, Sir Dru, was one of the warders of Mary, Queen of Scots, at Fotheringay, and afterwards Constable of the Tower. Sir Robert's manors and lands in Norfolk, Suffolk, Essex and Bucks. were divided amongst his children: and his estates in these parts were inherited by his son Robert.

There are memorials in the church to this Robert (died 1592) and his son Sir Henry Drury (died 1617). Henry was one of five Drury cousins knighted by James I before his coronation. Drury Lane in London takes its name from the family's town house. 'Drury House' was let for some time to Shakespeare's friend and patron, the Earl of Southampton, and it was there that Essex's rebellion was planned.[20] So we may imagine Sir Henry in the midst of that exciting London of Shakespeare's later years. His affairs in Chalfont St. Peter were capably managed, he added to his estates, and when he died left to his son William, then aged 20, extensive lands in these parishes, as well as a manor in Norfolk, and 'the Drury House and other houses in Drury Lane, in the parish of St. Clement Danes'.

But the first part of the seventeenth century was a particularly difficult time for the country gentry, and William was soon obliged to mortgage some parts of his estate and to sell others. (It may be that, like some other members of the Drury family, he also suffered as a Papist.) Even his mother's manor of Temple Bulstrode, which Sir Henry had settled on her when they married, was much diminished; and she retired to live with her daughter, Mrs John Penn, of Penn, where her memorial may be seen in the Church. We catch one further glimpse of William Drury when, in 1641, 'blind, lame, and destitute of estate', he made a pathetic appeal to the House of Lords against a mortgagee who had taken possession of Hedgerley Manor.[21]

He had sold in 1626 nearly all he had in Chalfont St. Peter and Hedgerley. The deed of sale, which marks the break-up of the estate, provides much interesting information about Chalfont St. Peter at that time. 'William Drury of Hedgerley Esq' sells to 'Henry Bulstrode of Horton Esq' for £13,900, the manor of Chalfont St. Peter, with the rectory, parsonage, tithes and advowson of the church; the manor of Brudenells, the Chantry of Whaplode, all the houses and lands called Mason (Marsham) End, Turvilles lands, the water-mill called Noke Mill etc. – except for certain leases specified. From these we learn that Thomas Baldwin has 'the Ould Place' at £150 p.a. (i.e. the old Brudenells manor house in 'Chalfont Park'), Mopes (4d) and Stampwell (£24); John Russell has Chalfont Lodge Farm, called the Tilehouse (£60); Richard Playter has Noke Mill, with lands and waters, at the substantial rent of £94 p.a.; the Playter family had also Bidwell's Wood, adjoining Mill Lane, and Gallows Wood beyond it; Robert Duck has the Grange, where his rent is £25, plus 1 qr. wheat, 1 qr. barley, 1 qr. oats, and entertainment for two days and one night twice yearly, for the lord and his retinue to keep court; Richard Whitchurch has Mumfords (£40), Thomas Tredway a farm called Butterfield's End, with 40 acres of Siblets Wood, and Richard Baker has both Dorsetts ('Marsham Farm') and a larger farm called Hatches (probably

'Latchmoor'). Robert Tibby rents the Greyhound, with 14 acres, for £22, and Thomas Franklin the Swan at £13 6s 8d, Richard Kirby has a blacksmith's shop (on Gold Hill) for which he pays £2 10s 0d and Robert Randall, a labourer, a cottage for which he must render each year three woodcocks.[22]

Some of the sixteenth and seventeenth century houses remain, notably Mumfords, Layters Farm, Holly Tree Farm,[23] Water Hall, Ashwells, Mopes and Hill Farm: others have been pulled down within living memory. The picture on page 19 shows some sixteenth and seventeenth century cottages near the church which were pulled down in 1933. It also shows (on the right, where the shopping centre now is) a larger seventeenth-century house, which stood in front of what used to be called 'Barrack Yard', into which a high covered gateway led. This interesting house was examined by Mr Clive Rouse in 1938 (when it was in process of demolition) who found there a complete scheme of mural paintings. (Amateur painters and house-decorators, please note!) There were several illuminated texts, a lively representation of David and Goliath, and a spirited painting of a unicorn. It was James I who introduced the Scottish unicorn into our Royal Arms, and this with the charming rose-and-thistle design found on the opposite wall, suggests that the owner was celebrating the Union of the English and Scottish Crowns in 1603.[24]

Inns

Whether his house was originally an inn or not, we know that in 1683 it was the Crossed Keys Inn, occupied by Tobias Goodridge at an annual rent of 2s 6d and taking its name, no doubt, from St. Peter's crossed keys; which brings us to the subject of inns. You noticed the 'Greyhound' and the 'Swan' in that deed of 1626. A list compiled in 1577 of innkeepers and alehouse keepers in Bucks gives the names of William Francklyn and William Noble, innkeepers in Chalfont St. Peter, and Richard Smythe, Ayleshouse-keeper. William Francklyn probably had the Swan; William Noble possibly the Greyhound.[25]

The Greyhound still stands: the Swan was opposite – only the barn remains, now ingeniously converted to the uses of the Youth Club. The Swan, of course, is the Bucks. emblem: the Greyhound was the Drury crest, so perhaps the 'Greyhound' originated with them. Richard Smith had the 'Bell' near the site of the present 'White Hart'. A *Catalogue of the Taverns in Tenne Shire about London*, published in 1636, mentions a tavern at 'Chaffant' kept by Robert Ducke. This was the 'Lion' – Lion Yard was a little above Joiners Lane. In 1683 we hear also of the 'Starr Inn' and the 'Five Bells', which, like the Crossed Keys and the Red Lion, were part of the manor of the vicarage.[26]

At Gerrards Cross, the earliest inn of which we have clear evidence is 'The Goat' (later the White Hart) which is mentioned in 1645, and stood a little west of the 'Bull'; but there was probably also an inn or ale-house where the 'French Horn' now stands. The Oxford Road was a dangerous road then (as it is still). In December 1691 'a waggon laden with their Majestyes' money was assaulted by several Thieves and Robbed', Joseph Perkyns, ostler 'at the Oxford Arms Inn at Gerrards Cross', 'going with Arms to defend it', was seriously wounded. He applied to the Justices for help in paying his doctor's bill, which they granted. The 'Oxford Arms' was evidently a predecessor of the 'Bull'.

In the following year Sir Roger Hill, of Denham Place, entered in his Justice's diary: 'Hue & Cry upon a robbery said to be committed last night near Gerrards Cross heath upon Robert Lord of Little Tue, Com. Oxon. yeoman, by two men, one a young man in a brown wig on a bay horse with a sprig tayle, ye other a short thick man on foot, both in blewish cloths, he swore he lost about 20s in silver, a pair of lead colored stokins, a sad coloured cloth riding coat several neck cloths & handkerchiefs & his silver sleeve buttons and his horse, being a bay with a blase in his face, the near foot being white, 15 hands high.'[27]

St. Peter's

Church and inn often went together in village life: and it is high time we looked at the church and its vicars. The church was not that which we see now, but an earlier building, which had already been altered and enlarged during the centuries, and evidently had two altars. When extensive repairs became necessary in 1965, many fragments of moulded stone of various periods, and of medieval timbers, were found, and the foundations of the earlier buildings were revealed.[28]

In the reign of Edward VI, careful enquiry was made concerning the goods of the churches (many of which were later seized by the Crown). In 1552, the Commissioners (Sir Robert Drury and others) agreed with the Churchwardens of St. Peter's, William Duck and Richard Taylor, an inventory of that Church's possessions. It is quite an impressive list, including three silver chalices with patens, two corporals (for carrying the reserved Sacrament), nine vestments (one 'of green velvet figured with daisies and birds'), four copes (one 'of blue bawdkyn with orfreys of nedill-worke') two copper-and-gilt crosses, two censers of latten, 'with a shippe', a pair of latten candlesticks for the high altar, 'one pair of organs', 'five bells in a ring' and 'one other litell bell commonly called the sanctus'. Whappelode's chantry had already been dissolved, and there remained 'no implements belonging to the said Chantry, but only one vestment for the priest to sing mass in, which is priced at 13s 4d and remaineth in the hands of Thomas Langshaw', the last chantry priest.[29]

Of the earlier vicars, most are little more than names to us (there is a list of them in the church), but occasionally we catch a glimpse of one, in the fields, in his manor court, or in the church. Remember that the vicar had considerable lands to farm; and one, at least, of them – John Bryan – also took on other lands. Probably they needed to, for the living was far from a fat one. According to a schedule of 1529, Francis Pollard the vicar, received £5 a year; Robert Semer, his curate, £6: and Thomas Langshaw, the chantry priest, £6. A brass representing a priest in mass vestments commemorates Robert Hanson, who was the vicar at the time the Abbey came to an end, and also vicar of Little Missenden. It would seem that he was a Yorkshireman, for in his will he remembered the churches of Duffield and Holmfirth, near Huddersfield, as well as the churches and the poor of Chalfont St. Peter and Missenden. (He also, by the way, bequeathed to a cousin at Oxford 'a standing rote' – a kind of lyre.)[30]

These were difficult times for churchmen, who were required to acknowledge, as Head of the Church, the Pope, imperious Henry, Protestant Edward, Catholic Mary, and middle-of-the-road Elizabeth, all within the space of one generation. Hanson's predecessor Roger Edgeworth, for his anti-Protestant sentiments, gained rapid preferment, and became Chancellor of Bath and Wells; Hanson's successor, Thomas Slitherst, the first President of Trinity College, Oxford, for his anti-Protestant sentiments, was deprived of his living.[31]

Queen Elizabeth wanted to know not only that the church services were being observed with due order, but also that the church was playing its important part in the urgent task of poor relief. Thus our churchwardens of 1601 report: 'It may please you to understand by these present that our neighbours do in reasonable good sort repair to the church, and further we have given a stock of corn to the use of the poor which cometh to the sum of £20 and upwards, and withal there is a second supply for the relief of the poor which cometh to the sum 9s by the week, which is weekly to be distributed.'

The vicarage, next to the church, was already a sizeable house, consisting of 'five bays built of timber and covered with tiles', with hall, kitchen, parlour, and seven rooms above, and several outhouses and barns, some tiled, some thatched, a little garden next to the churchyard and a glebe meadow with some fruit trees. The other glebe lands were the fields running westwards from the church between the parish boundary and Common Down, three fields called Goldhill Closes (behind the site of 'Rock House') and some pieces in the common fields – in all about 60 acres.[32]

Fulmer and its New Church

Here let us look across the border and salute Fulmer Church and its builder. Fulmer manor, which for much of its long history had belonged to the owner of Stoke Poges, had been granted in 1606, 'for service of one rose', to Sir Marmaduke Darrell. Marmaduke Darrell was for more than forty years Victualler to the Navy, responsible for supplying not only food and drink but many things beside. He was well acquainted with Drake and Hawkins and the other sea-captains of the time, and a member of the Council which planned the expedition against Spain. He was with the fleet at Plymouth on a memorable day in July 1588, when he and the mayor, looking out, saw on the horizon the Spanish galleons approaching, and was able to send a message to the Queen that Lord Howard had led out the English fleet to engage the Armada.

The latter part of his long life saw a phenomenal rise in the demand for coal in and around London; and Sir Marmaduke, with two or three of his colleagues, secured the contract for carrying coals from Newcastle, with a royalty of 12d on every chaldron.

This was the distinguished Civil Servant who had come to live at Fulmer. He built a new manor house there, on the beautiful site now occupied by Fulmer Place, acquired other properties in the neighbourhood, and showed himself a generous patron to the village.

Old Fulmer Church, nearly a mile further up the valley, was in a sad state of disrepair, and the villagers found the path to it very miry: and so Sir Marmaduke Darrell, the lord of the manor, gave them a new church. It was consecrated on All Saints Day 1610, and it contains a fine memorial to Sir Marmaduke and his family, with an inscription relating that he was Victualler to the Navy in the days of the first Queen Elizabeth, and Cofferer (Paymaster) to James I and Charles I, and 'was favoured by all these renowned princes and employed in matters of great trust for the space of fifty years, in all which he acquitted himself with credit and commendation'. There are few English churches of this period, and St. James Fulmer, is certainly a beautiful example.[33]

Puritans and Laudians

But now the battle is mounting between High Church and Puritan, mingled with the battle between King and Parliament. James Bradshaw, who was vicar in 1626, when Henry Bulstrode bought the living, was a Laudian. 'Laudian' we must say now, for already the most powerful force in the bench of bishops is William Laud, pious, industrious, and ruthless, soon to become Archbishop of Canterbury. Laud set himself to enforce decent and uniform standards in doctrines, services and buildings. A thorough enquiry made in 1637 revealed the deplorable condition of many of the church buildings. (It gives us, by the way, one of our very few glimpses of the private chapel at Hedgerley Bulstrode: 'There is a loft round about it above, to look into it through the lattice casements.' St. Peter's Church fares better than some others: evidently something had been done since it was reported in 1612 that one side was 'so broken that a hog may creep through'. In 1637, there are still some holes – in the steeple. Inside the church are some high family pews that will have to be cut down (a very common complaint). The rood-loft door behind the pulpit is 'to be stopt up handsomely', and the Communion table needs improvement. Two flagons, a new chalice, and a poor man's box, are to be provided. The register, we are told, dates from 28 March 1538.[34]

But dilapidated buildings were not Laud's major problem: he had also to deal with refractory parsons and people. Buckinghamshire since the days of the Lollards had been noted for nonconformity, and at this time had many Puritan ministers and gentry, including the influential John Hampden. Laud had a loyal supporter in Dr John Andrews, the Rector of Beaconsfield, who writes to the Archbishop:

'They keep up their brabblings and janglings in our church about election of officers, and their accounts, and every base matter: yea, and keep their musters, or inspection of arms, in our churchyard. Many gad from church to church on Sundays to hear Puritanical sermons in other churches, contrary to the law. Few or none come to Church on Holy Days in all the year, not even the churchwardens. Many sit at divine service with their hats on, and some lie along the pews, their heads covered, even at the Litany or the Ten Commandments.'

It was decided to make an example of some of the Puritan parsons, and the Archbishop's Commissioner, when he held his Visitation at Amersham in 1635, suspended from office the reverend Elkanah Gladman of Chesham, and the reverend Thomas Valentine of Chalfont St. Giles.

On Christmas Day that year there was a scandalous affair at Fulmer. Gervase Good, the constable of Chalfont St. Peter, was alleged to have arrested someone for debt in the church, in the course of the Communion Service. Dr Andrews, reporting, seizes the occasion to express once more his concerns. Gervase Good denied that he had arrested the man in Church: he 'only whispered him in the ear, and carried him to Gerrards Cross, and there did arrest him'. But others told a different tale, and Dr Andrews concludes that Good was at fault: but adds that it may be said in extenuation that 'the people here-abouts had been so mistaught that they did not think Sunday, or even Christmas Day, more sacred that any other day, or the Church a place of greater holiness or respect than stables or barns'. 'In the meantime give me leave to tell you that you yourself are banned and cursed to the pit of hell for suspending Mr Valentine of St. Giles Chalfont and Mr Gladman ... Or thus (as I hear) the women talk up and down these parts. The men put in their horns and their tongues too.'[35]

The men did not all restrain their tongues. One Isaac Penington had come to live at Chalfont St. Peter at the Grange. Much of the history of Chalfont St. Peter might be written around the story of the Grange (now the Holy Cross Convent). Through all the years that Missenden Abbey held the manor, the Grange was its 'Manor house' in Chalfont St. Peter, where the Abbot's court was held, and the Abbot's bailiff lived. In Edmund Brudenell's time (as we have seen) it was allowed to fall into a sad state of disrepair, but the Drurys had evidently put it into better shape, and now, in 1637, Henry Bulstrode had sold it, and extensive lands with it, to a relative by marriage, 'Isaac Penington of London esq.'[36]

Penington was a remarkable man, one of the key figures in the turbulent history of that time, when both King and Parliament were bidding for the support of the City of London. An out-and-out Parliament man, as a substantial citizen, a leading alderman (Lord Mayor in 1642) and one of the City's representatives in the Long Parliament, he was a living and fiery link between the Puritans in Parliament, in the City government, and amongst the citizens at large. A sincerely religious man, he served as a vestry-man in the famous Puritan church of St. Stephen's, Coleman Street, and was well acquainted with all the Puritan leaders, and an implacable opponent of the policies of Archbishop Laud.[37]

This was the gentleman who had taken the Grange as a country house. He did not find his parish church congenial. One of his complaints was that there was no Sunday afternoon 'lecture'; and when the vicar, Mr Bradshaw, replied that the Archbishop had forbidden such lectures, Penington had some plain words to say about the Archbishop. He also had a gardener, after his own heart, who did not scruple to argue theology with his vicar.

Poor Mr Bradshaw! Laud's power was waning: and our vicar chose this unfortunate moment to utter some of his most extravagant remarks, declaring that 'the bishops' courts were the suburbs of heaven, and their officers the very supremacies next to archangels: and that to refuse to appear before them, or to use any but the Book

36

of Common Prayer, or to preach twice on a Sunday, were all damnable sins'.[38] He was soon afterwards deprived of his living, by order of the House of Commons, and the reverend Thomas Holl came to be our vicar in his stead – of whom more later.[39]

Roundheads and Cavaliers

Mr Holl came to us about the time of the beginning of the Civil War, that unhappy conflict that caused much misery and divided many families. We were mostly Roundheads. Henry Bulstrode was appointed to raise the Trained Bands throughout the Chiltern Hundred, with Henry Gould of Oak End as one of his lieutenants, and young George Fleetwood of the Vache raised a troop of horse; and we may be sure that some of our men went with them. Troops and rumours travelled along the high road, between the King's headquarters at Oxford, and Parliament's HQ in London: High Wycombe was a kind of frontier town, and Beaconsfield a rallying point for the Parliament forces. In November 1642 came 'joyful news' of the victory of the parliamentary forces over Prince Rupert near Aylesbury; and in the following August, Essex himself rode through 'Chaffant' at the head of 7,000 men, making a wide detour round Oxford, on his way to the relief of Gloucester. 'On March 23, 1643, the Earl Carnarvon and Price Rupert with other great ones, marched to Wendover and plundered all the towns thereabouts.' But we saw little of the actual fighting, and for the most part, we just carried on, grumbling because we were short-handed, because horses and wagons and stocks had been commandeered, and because taxes were heavy, for wars cost money. At last came news of the crowning victory of Worcester, and we saw Cromwell himself pass through, on his way to Westminster, driving a horde of Scottish prisoners before him.[40]

In Commonwealth times, great changes in church and state were made – on paper: how far they affected the lives of ordinary folk varied from place to place. One regulation which was much resented discouraged marriages in church; and indeed, our parish register records few marriage in this period. Parliament did, at least, increase our vicar's stipend by £33 a year. Mr Holl remained our vicar from 1643 to 1679, contriving not to be turned out by either party, keeping the respect of his people, and dying, as he lived, a poor man. His son Richard became a shoemaker in Chesham, and it is pleasant to find that, not long before he died in 1679, the old man was able to baptize his great-grandson there.[41]

Early Quakers

How did Mr Holl cope, one wonders, with some very nonconforming Non-conformists in his parish? In 1654 Alderman Penington's son, another Isaac Penington, had married a well-to-do widow, Lady Mary Springett, and they had come to live at the Grange, with her daughter Gulielma. Much against his father's wishes, Isaac and his wife had turned Quakers, and their house soon became a meeting-place for Friends from far and near. George Fox himself was there in 1658, about the time of Cromwell's death: and the young Thomas Ellwood came to visit them, and at a meeting at the Grange first saw the Light. Thereafter he was a frequent visitor, and eventually stayed as tutor to the Penington children. The Quakers were always in trouble; they did not attend their parish church, nor pay tithes, nor doff their hats, and they would not take an oath; when all 'conventicles' were forbidden, they continued to meet for worship. In consequence, many of them spent years in and out of filthy seventeenth-century prisons. Isaac Penington spent several periods in Aylesbury gaol, generally in the company of such other local stalwarts as George Salter and Henry Tredway of Hedgerley, and William Russell of Jordans Farm.

Ellwood, in his admirable autobiography, tells how he brought a visitor to the Grange – a middle-aged Independent named John Okey – on a day in 1661, when it happened that leading Friends from other parts of the country were present. On the Sunday morning, they were gathered at their silent meeting, when suddenly they heard the clatter of horses, and a party of soldiers rode up to the house. 'We all sat still in our place, except John Okey, who sat next to me. But he, being of a profession that approved Peter's advice to his Lord "to save himself" soon took the alarm, and with the nimbleness of a stripling, cutting a caper over a form that stood before him, ran quickly out at a private door, which led through the parlour into the gardens, and thence into an orchard, where he hid himself in a place so secure, and withal so convenient for his intelligence by observation of what passed, that no one of the family could have found a likelier.'

Meanwhile, the soldiers tramped in. The officer in charge was civil enough, but his orders were to break up the meeting, and to take the leaders before a magistrate. So to Denham Court they trudged, to appear before Sir William Bowyer. Sir William examined them, and decided he must commit them to prison; but each time his clerk drafted a mittimus, the Friends found some flaw in it. At length, the exasperated magistrate sent them home, telling them they would hear from him in the morning. Returning to the Grange, they found Mary Penington and the other Friends still sitting in the meeting, and amongst them a very shame-faced John Okey.

Another story Ellwood tells is of a Quaker funeral procession at Amersham, which was rudely interrupted by an important-looking gentleman, who rushed out of an inn, sword in hand. This was

Ambrose Bennett Esq. of Hedgerley Bulstrode, a magistrate. He
laid about him with the flat of his sword, sent the coffin tumbling to
the ground, and ordered the constables to arrest these men. When
another magistrate had been found – Sir Thomas Clayton of the
Vache – the Quakers were once more committed to Aylesbury gaol.

It was during Penington's fourth spell in prison that a heavy blow
fell on the family. Old Alderman Penington, who had been one of
Charles I's judges, had been imprisoned in the Tower (where he
died) and all his estates confiscated, and now the younger Isaac and
his family were evicted from the Grange. They found refuge for a
time at Bottrells Farm, Chalfont St. Giles, and afterwards at Bury
Farm, Amersham.

But the rest of these things – how in the Plague Year, Thomas
Ellwood found a cottage at Chalfont St. Giles for his blind friend
and tutor, John Milton, how William Penn took Gulielma Springett
in marriage at King's Farm, Chorleywood, how in 1688 Jordan's
Meeting House was built (with William Grimsdale of Maltman's
Green as one of its trustees) – these things have been told elsewhere
– and we must leave them with special salute to those indomitable
ladies, Mary Penington and Gulielma Penn, and a remembrance of
our other local stalwarts. When the Archdeacon carried out his
Visitation in 1662, nine persons in Chalfont St. Peter were reported
for non-attendance at church. Besides Isaac Penington and his wife,
they were George and Rebecca Salter, Edward Barton and his wife,
John Monk, Mary, wife of Henry Watkins (of the Red Lion) and the
wife of William Grassingham. All (except Monk) are identifiable as
Quakers.[42]

Two Silver Spoons

Some of the men and women of those days we catch sight of for a
moment when they appear in a court of law – or when they write
their wills, wills that take us back to times when possessions were few
and precious. Thomas Butterfield, yeoman, bequeathes to his
daughter Marie 'the two silver spoons given to my first wife on her
marriage day', and to his two sons 'six dozen silver buttons'. Richard
Playtor of Noke Mill, miller, leaves to his granddaughter Elizabeth 'a
cubbard standing in my bed chamber, and her grandmother's
gowne'. Thomas Wetherley, of Tubbs Farm, bequeathes to his wife,
besides their bed and other household goods, 'one brown cow, and
one hogge of bacon which is in the chimney'. John Monk,
husbandman, leaves each of his grandchildren a lamb. Neighbourly
Sibbell Cawdry, widow, leaves 'a pair of sheets apiece to Good-wife
Craft and Goodwife Nashe, one sheet each to Widow Charsley and
Widow Batchelor', and 10s 'to the poor that dwell at this end of the

town'. Gervase Good ('Jarvis Goade' it is spelt) – whom we met earlier, creating a disturbance in Fulmer church – remembers all his children, but had evidently a special fondness for his youngest, Frances, who is to have 'three pewter dishes, the best coverlet, a blanket, my flock-bed, one joyned bedstead, one feather bolster, one feather pillow, a pillow-beere, one brass porridge-pot, one high joyned stool, a boulting-tub, a corne-tub, two pairs of sheets, two table napkins, one diaper napkin', and £8 when she reaches the age of 18. 'And whereas William Eastwood the elder, of Chalfont, did out of his goodwill offer to be at the charge of one barrel of beer at my burial, I give to the said William my best green suit, my doublet and hose, my short coat and green stockings, my garters and girdle, and my best hat.'[43]

The Church House Affair

Others we may meet on the occasion of a village row. The manor of Chalfont St. Peter had been bought in 1650 by a prosperous local farmer, Richard Whitchurch, of Mumfords (and Mumfords remained the 'Manor House' for 300 years.)[44] He does not seem to have been very popular in the village. Near the church stood an old building called the Church House, which the villagers had always thought of as belonging to the parish. In days gone by, they had had their Whitsun and Midsummer Ales there, junketings at which a good time was had by all, and a little money raised for the church. Now Richard Whitchurch has let it, at £3 a year, to a young butcher, John Copland, who has his shop there, and his slaughter-house behind, next to the church. The villagers protested, and at an enquiry held at Amersham in September 1665, a verdict was given in their favour: Richard Whitchurch is to pay over £20 of rent, release and quitclaim and premises to the vicar and churchwardens, and pay costs. But Richard appealed, and a further enquiry was held in the following August at the Red Lion in Chalfont St. Peter, kept by Joseph Freer.

The oldest inhabitant is brought out – Eldred Newman, said to be 'about a hundred years old'. But he maintained that it was the lord of the manor who had had the letting of the house in the past, and had repaired it; and added that Church Ales had been discontinued 'by reason of the disorders that usually fell out after them'. John Newman, yeoman, aged 60, remembered that when he and three other young men wanted to keep a Midsummer Ale, they gave the churchwardens 20s to have it in the Church House. Winloe Grimsdell of 'Hugerley', added that the lord used to contribute a bushel of wheat and an angel in money. Thomas Egleton, 36, husbandman, remembered that a school used to be kept in the house, and that sometimes poor people were allowed to occupy part of it. John Monk, weaver, aged 39, said that his father used to live there, as Mr William Drury said he might, provided he paid no rent: he used to give the churchwardens 4s a year to keep the church clock in repair. Since then 'an ancient woman' had occupied it, but she had now been removed to an almshouse. But John Well, husbandman, maintained that poor people had been obliged to leave it, because they could not 'lye dry'. And John Aldridge and Ralph Cock, bricklayers and carpenters, gave evidence that they had repaired it at Mr Whitchurch's expense, which cost him £18. However, Robert Dell, aged 54, parish clerk, produced the ancient parish books, as kept by his father, who had been parish clerk before him: and the records and figures seem to have carried most weight with the jurors. The vicar and churchwardens appear to have won in the end, for a few years later 'Two Church Houses' are mentioned amongst their possessions.[45]

Enter St. John's College

The King had come home, and most Englishmen were glad of it. The Restoration Year was marked by one event which has had lasting influence upon our village life. Sir Thomas Allen of Finchley had bought the living of the church in 1645 from Colonel Thomas Bulstrode, and in 1660, grateful for the King's return, and grateful to his old college, he gave it to St. John's College, Oxford, who have ever since presented the vicars of St. Peter's. The college has two rather charming notes from the good man. The first is in acknowledgement of their letter of thanks:

'I heartily thank you and your society for your gracious acceptance of my love. Mr Holl, the vicar, shall send you the £20 due ... The living yielded £60 this year, I am informed: but sometimes the fall of timber doth much better it. I should be better satisfied if it were more proportionate to my desires and your merit. But the Lord be Praised that gave it to me to give it unto you. So presenting my service to your much-honoured self and college, I rest, your servant, Thomas Allen.'

The other relates to some arrears of tithes:

'Your under-tenant at Chalfont St. Peter wants authority to sue some for arrears of tithes. He must do it now in the name of the college. They were never sued yet: but I know their constitution so well, that I assure you a little bit of green wax will do more with them than 104 sermons from the vicar yearly ... The Lord preserve you and yours here and eternally. So prayeth, Sir, your true friend and servant, Thos. Allen.'[46]

Mr Dudley Rewse

The King had come home; and there were jobs to be had. Mr Dudley Rewse, who had acquired Brudenells Manor, and was on good terms with the Darrells of Fulmer and the Palmers of Dorney, in 1665 secured the post of bailiff and paymaster of Windsor Castle (the King remarking that his predecessor had 'in his proportion cheated beyond any accountant'). The castle was evidently much in need of repair, and Rewse was authorised to spend £1,000 on it. Soon afterwards he added another office, that of Receiver of Royal Aid for the Treasurer of the Navy in the Country of Oxford. But the authorities were already discovering their mistake. Try as they would, they could not get Mr Rewse's account from him. When eventually he was arrested and brought to book, he was found to owe the King £18,889. He seems soon to have been at liberty again and died at Chalfont St. Peter in 1675. A certain obscurity which hangs over the history of Brudenells in this period arises largely from the many claims of creditors upon his estate. It was not until 1688 that James II decided (no doubt with a little prompting) that he might as well write off the debt still owing to the Crown, and that the man who had most claim to Dudley Rewse's estate in Chalfont was George, Lord Jeffreys.[47]

Judge Jeffreys

These villages have had many notable residents, but perhaps only one whose name everyone knows – Judge Jeffreys. A Welshman of the Welshmen, who claimed descent from Tudor Trevor, an eleventh-century Lord of Hereford, young George Jeffreys, when in 1663 he was admitted to the Inner Temple, found kinsman there before him. An older cousin, Arthur Trevor, helped him and gave him the run of his chambers; and his first-cousin, John Trevor, had lately been called to the Bar. But George soon leaped ahead by his own charm, ability and pushfulness. At the age of 25 he was elected Common Serjeant of the City of London, and five years later was knighted and took silk.

Arthur Trevor had bought the Grange at Chalfont St. Peter in 1665, and two years later his nephew John inherited it. (This is the Sir John Trevor who became Master of the Rolls and Speaker in the House of Commons, and was said to have been as pure in the former capacity as he was corrupt in the latter.)[48] He adopted the Grange as his country house – his son Tudor Trevor was baptised in St. Peter's Church – and it was probably through visits to him that Jeffreys first became interested in this neighbourhood, and on the death of Ambrose Bennett of Hegerley Bulstrode, bought that estate from Bennett's widow and nephew. In the summer and autumn of 1676 he had a small army of labourers, glaziers, carpenters, masons and bricklayers at work, fitting up the mansion for his reception. There are builders' accounts for work 'don at Bulstrod House' and 'the letell house at Jarats Cras' (probably the original of 'Raylands Mead'). Amongst the materials used were £45-worth of bricks '2 iron cullums', '67 foot of Dutch tyles', 'Packthred', and '3,000 Lath nayles'. One contractor's bill came to over £70, to which he added: '14 weeks for myself-what you please'. Jeffrey's bailiff at Bulstrode at this time appears to have been Henry Tredway the Quaker, and one likes to imagine the two together.[49]

Jeffreys' wife died whilst the work was in progress. He had married for love a poor parson's daughter, and was devoted to her, and this must have been a sore loss to him. We know that he was at Bulstrode in August 1678, for in that month Charles II and some of his court drove over from Windsor and dined there, and the King was so affable as to cause his host to 'sit down at the table with him' and 'drank to him seven times'.

Elections

Jeffreys' promotion continued to be rapid and he soon became Lord Chief Justice, and a man to be feared. High Wycombe, for example, hastened to elect him Lord High Steward, thanked him profusely for his acceptance, and put up his coat of arms in the Guildhall. But he did not have things all his own way in Bucks. Macaulay tells the story of the election of a Member of Parliament for the county in 1685, when Jeffreys was determined to oust the Whig candidate, Thomas Wharton. The Tories tried to outwit the Whigs by switching the polling at the last moment from Aylesbury to Newport Pagnell, and both parties poured out large sums in bribes: but 'the stout-hearted yeomen of Bucks.' rallied round, and Jeffreys' candidate was heavily defeated.[50]

'Your Money or Your Life'

There are several tales of highwaymen associated with Bulstrode. The most circumstantial tells how a notorious highwayman called 'Old Mobb' stopped Lord Chief Justice Jeffreys not far from his house, disabled the two coachmen, and demanded money. 'Do you know who I am, sirrah?' asked Jeffreys. 'Yes, sir,' answered Old Mobb, 'I know you very well: and I ought by rights to charge you with a constable, for you once put me in great danger of my life – at Hertford Assizes. But I'm resolved to be even with you now'. At which, with a dreadful oath, he threatened to shoot, and the Lord Chief Justice handed over what money he had.[51]

Bulstrode Rebuilt

It was not until later, after he had become Lord Chancellor at the age of forty, that Jeffreys rebuilt Bulstrode, which is said to have been badly damaged by fire in or about 1685. Tradition says that he lived at the Grange whilst it was being rebuilt, and this may well be true, for he had bought that house from his cousin Trevor five years earlier. He also bought, from Sir Roger Hill of Denham, the manor of Temple Bulstrode, thus uniting the two Bulstrode manors – Hedgerley Bulstrode and Temple Bulstrode.[52] The County Record Office has in its keeping a map of his estate prepared for him in 1686 by one John Fisher, which, besides being a beautiful example of the map-maker's art, is of great topographical interest, showing the houses, the roads, and the field names. For example, it shows Gerrards 'Cross' as the spot where the main road from Chalfont St. Peter to Windsor crossed the Oxford road, a road that now survives only as a footpath across Bulstrode Park, from Main Drive to the Hedgerley Lane gate, continuing by Mounthill Lane to Stoke Poges and Windsor.

The engraving reproduced on page iv shows the gardens and the south front of Bulstrode substantially as it was built for Jeffreys. This imposing front, built of brick, extended 200 feet, with the principal rooms above, the bedrooms below. Behind it were two courts, separated by the hall of the old Tudor manor house. Looking into the first court, and extending across its whole width, was what Horace Walpole called 'a brave gallery of old pictures'. From the end of this gallery opened the chapel, where in October 1687 Jeffreys' daughter Margaret was married, and in July of the following year his only surviving son John, a wild lad of 15, married Lady Charlotte Herbert, daughter of the Earl of Pembroke. The King and his counsellors wore wedding favours to celebrate the day, and a month later James II and his Queen, Mary of Modena, came to dine at Bulstrode.[53]

The end came quickly. In December the King fled the country, and Jeffreys was arrested, when trying to make his escape, and was imprisoned in the Tower, where he died in the following April. In his will, written in the Tower, he protests his undying loyalty to the Church of England, 'which I take to be the best Church in the world', and he expresses his anxiety for his children.[54]

Dutch Hans

Jeffreys might well have been anxious concerning his son 'Jacky' who got through a considerable fortune in a few years, and was heavily in debt when he died in 1702. Four years later, his sister and her husband sold Bulstrode to a greater if less colourful personality – Hans William Bentinck, the Dutchman who had been the ever-faithful servant and friend of William, Prince of Orange, had nursed him through smallpox, suffered many wounds in his campaigns, become his most trusted diplomatic adviser, been the chief manager of the invasion in 1688, and had been created Earl of Portland and Viscount Woodstock when William and his wife Mary became King and Queen of England.[55]

Bentinck does not seem to have altered Bulstrode, save to complete the wings, shown in the view on page i, which Jeffreys had begun. He laid out the formal gardens, probably with the assistance of Henry Wise, who had served under him on the Royal Gardens, and added the Long Water, reminiscent of his Dutch canals. To him we owe that straight stretch of the Windsor Road between the Packhorse and Hedgerley Lane. There is a document in the County Record Office, containing the signatures of a large number of local residents in 1707, consenting to his straightening the narrow and twisty road to Windsor 'by Widow Lane's Farm'.[56] Nor let it be forgotten that he gave Gerrards Cross its first school, in Bull Lane, 'where are taught 20 boys and 15 girls, and all of them clothed: two of the Children are put out Apprentice each year'. The Earl endowed it with £40 per annum – £20 for the schoolmaster, £20 for the schoolmistress.[57]

Bentinck, who was unhappily estranged from the King in his later years, and was never very popular with the English people, had resigned most of his public offices. But he was able to enjoy some years of comparative peace and domestic happiness at Bulstrode, at the close of his strenuous life. There his two youngest children were born; there in 1707 his daughter Frances married Lord Byron; there in 1708, Queen Anne visited him; and there in 1709 he died.[58]

His son, the second Earl, and afterwards first Duke of Portland – who also bought the Grange and its lands from Jeffreys' heirs – was responsible for a notable redecoration of the Chapel at Bulstrode, a complete scheme of Venetian wall-paintings, executed by Sebastiano Ricci, one of the Italian painters who came to England to take part in the competition for the decoration of the dome of the newly completed St. Paul's Cathedral.[59]

The Fall of the Church

We must return to the village of Chalfont St. Peter, upon which a sad calamity has fallen. One morning in July 1708, in a time of high winds and heavy rain, the tower of the church crashed onto the nave and aisles (one suspect that those holes noted 70 years earlier had never been thoroughly repaired). The vicar and churchwardens, surveying the ruins, evidently decided that the best course was to clear them away and start afresh. They were given leave to send out an appeal to all the parishes round about; but the money trickled in slowly: in January 1710, All Saints Hertford, sent £2 6s 0d and six months later, St. Paul's Walden, contributed 1s 3d. Browne Willis, the Bucks. antiquary, who visited Chalfont St. Peter at this time, found the church still in ruins, and the vicar, the reverend Thomas Smart, bravely carrying on services in the chancel. What happened to the fabric of the old church – apart from those few stones now in the porch – does not appear; no doubt some was used in the foundations, and some in the tower, of the present church; other pieces have cropped up from time to time in private gardens.

Plans were prepared for a new church, rather smaller than the old one (there were only 100 families in the parish) and at last building was begun. A summary of the final accounts survives:

Joiners work	... ...	£100		
Blacksmiths	... ...	20		
Plummers	... ...	100		
Glaziers	... ...	10		
Brickers	... ...	641	2	6
Carpenters	... ...	650	3	–
Total	... ...	£1521	5	6

Eventually, in 1714, a handsome new Queen Anne church was completed and consecrated. The mellowed tower and west end still proclaim its beauty, but the east end was altered, and not improved, in the 1850s.[60]

Oakend and Marsham Lodge

Among the local gentry who contributed to the rebuilding, we may notice especially Henry Gould and John Wilkins.

Henry Gould was the fourth of the name to live at Oak End. His uncle (as mentioned above) was active for Parliament in the Civil War; and this Henry was born in the time of the Commonwealth, married Deborah, daughter of Thomas Whitchurch, Lord of the Manor of Chalfont St. Peter, and lived to become an eighteenth-century Squire, Justice of the Peace, and High Sheriff in 1704. He appears to have rebuilt Oak End about the turn of the century. Ever a staunch Whig and a faithful churchman, he is described on his memorial in the church as 'amantissimus, utilissimus'.[61]

The parish register for 1700 records the baptism of 'Charles, son

THE BULL HOTEL, GERRARD'S CROSS.

Above: the Bull Hotel, c. 1900, and, below: a view across West Common, from about the position of the playing field, towards the Bull Hotel, which can be seen in the background with the cricket pitch in between.

Above: an aerial view of East Common and the Oxford Road, looking west, late 1920, with the French Horn to the left, the Apple Tree to the right and St James's Church in the distance. The following year the Common was devastated by a fire (there had also been one in 1911). Below: A view of the pond at the edge of the Oxford Road on the Common, looking towards the houses of West Common.

Above: a view of St Hubert's Cottages, East Common, from the A40, before the telephone lines were channeled underground, and below: Marsham Lane viewed from Oak End Way towards the railway bridge, a card postmarked April 1916. Sadly no photographs seem to exist of Lovell's small buildings that were pulled down to build the large block of offices between Station Road and the bridge, (their head office until 1999), which consisted of a row of small buildings (across the road from which the Rev. Geoffrey Edmonds lived for many years), each with a different style of roofing to help prospective clients to decide on the type of tiles they wished to use. The twentieth century residential housing of Gerrards Cross was very much the product of Y.J.Lovell, builders. Since this picture was taken a row of elms grew tall to the right, by Station Road, all of which were stricken by Dutch Elm Disease.

MARSHAM LANE, GERRARD'S CROSS.

SOUTH PARK, GERRARD'S CROSS.

Above: the Park Creamery, between South Park and Oak End Way, which was demolished in 1968, and below: The Parade (now part of Packhorse Road), 1908, a few years before the building that was for so many years the Barclays Bank (now W.R.Beck, property managers) and the National Westminster Bank buildings (originally the London County and Westminster Bank) were there. The stores became the site of the County Garage, and the building advertising Augustus Gibbons, later Gibbons & Clarke, then Giddy & Giddy, remained until 1983 when it was demolished and replaced by the present building presently occupied by Hamptons. None of the buildings facing these were built until c. 1920.

Above: the same block, when it had been largely taken over by the County Garage. Below: Packhorse Road used only to be the stretch of road between the railway line and the Oxford Road, but it later took over The Parade, and the stretch of road between it and Austenwood Common. The view here is from the railway bridge looking towards the Packhorse. The present Post Office was only built in 1913. Prior to that it was the other side of Marsham Way, in the premises (presently occupied by Brown & Merry) with a tailor's shop.

Above: that part of Packhorse Road known as Station Parade, c. 1920, at the corner of Station Road with the London County & Westminster Bank (now the National Westminster Bank) in the foreground, and the erstwhile Barclay's Bank building in the distance. Before moving to this imposing edifice, Barclay's was in the building at the corner of Station Road and Packhorse Road, at the right of this photograph. Below: the view from the Bulstrode Way/Marsham Way crossroads by the Post Office towards the railway bridge. The east side of Packhorse Road from Oak End Way to Marsham Way, and the west side from the Packhorse Inn to Bulstrode Way was known as Station Parade (or just The Parade); between Bulstrode Way and the railway line were the homes of the Railway's employees, Railway Cottages and Station House (the Station Master's), while the section from Station Approach to the Ethorpe Hotel was known as The Highway.

Gerrards Cross, Station Parade

Above: an archery contest in the 1950s in the grounds of Marsham Lodge, before it was pulled down c. 1966, and the Span houses were built on the site. Below: The Parade (also known as Station Parade), 1908, viewed from the corner opposite Ethorpe House (now the Hotel), towards the railway line. At this time the London County and Westminster Bank site was still a bare patch of land, and Barclay's Bank was still in the building facing it.

The Parade, Gerrards Cross.

Above: the men who built St James's Church, Gerrards Cross, 1859. Below: The Gerrards Cross Fire Brigade and engine, with its driver, George Newman, c. 1939. The fire station was in Oak End Way, and until it moved to its present location on the Oxford Road in Tatling End in 1983, all its members were volunteers.

Above: members of the Old Berkeley Hunt on a stage coach, outside the Bull Hotel, c. 1926. Below: pit-propping behind the French Horn public house, off the Oxford Road, during the first World War. This area, Fulmer Common, now known as Dukes Wood, had been common land until enclosed by Act of Parliament at the petition of the 12th Duke of Somerset.

Above: the houses at the end of West Common, with Latchmoor Pond in the foreground. The largest house, on the extreme right of the picture, now known as Walpole House (its owner, Mr J.J. Smit having renamed it after HMS Walpole, the ship that collected him and most of the Dutch diamond merchants' stock at a North Sea rendezvous at the time of the German invasion of the Netherlands) was prior to that called Latchmoor House (not to be confused with the present building of that name), and was the childhood home of Audrey Baker, author of *The History of Bulstrode*. For a time in the 19th century it had been called Bellevue House. Below: An aerial view of the Bull Hotel, c. 1920.

Above and below: exterior and plaster ceiling of Woodhill, on the Oxford Road, in ruinous state, c. 1970. This building with its Adams staircase and ceilings was deliberately allowed to fall into ruin so it could be demolished. An attempt to buy and restore the house in 1968, when it was in much better condition than shown here and still partly furnished, was frustrated by the owner's solicitors who insisted that as they had planning permission to build three houses on the site they would not sell Woodhill for less than the going rate for three plots. The Woodhill Farm Estate – most of the land bounded by the A40, A413, Mill Lane and East Common – had been bought from Brazenose College Oxford in 1894 by Col. the Hon. W. Le P. Trench, who lived at St Hubert's. When the Farm was divided up for sale in 1923, Lot 6 was bought by C.P.Lovell for development as the present Woodhill Estate.

An aerial view of Gerrards Cross, looking north, c. 1926, bisected by the railway line.

Packhorse Road, looking north from the Packhorse Inn, in 1975. The Congregational Church, of which the Rev. G.C. Edmonds had been minister from 1950 to 1972, was later pulled down and replaced by the present place of worship over a row of shops. This photograph was taken very early one summer morning by Clive Lloyd.

of John Wilkins, ironmonger, of Westminster'. John appears to have had a lease of the Grange from about 1700; but in 1714 he acquired the Chalfont Park estate. It was he who built Marsham Lodge, opposite Gerrards Cross Common, about 1727, apparently as a dower-house, on part of land called Walters Croft. (On another part of the same land a house was built, a few years later, where the Memorial Centre now stands.) He also had a house in Pall Mall, which, after his death in 1740, his widow let to Lord Berkeley of Stratton. She, we are told, had been a Miss Mary Drake, a distant relative of John Churchill, the great Duke of Marlborough, who had introduced her into the household of Queen Anne, with whom she had been a great favourite.[62]

Churchills at Chalfont

Not long after her death, a nearer relative of Marlborough came to Chalfont. The Duke had a nephew, General Charles Churchill, who was much enamoured of a celebrated actress of the day, Ann Oldfield, by whom he had a son, another Charles Churchill. This Charles married in 1748 Lady Maria Walpole, Sir Robert Walpole's daughter by Maria Skerrett, the Irish charmer whom he subsequently married. The trustees of General Churchill's will bought for them, for £7,600, the manor of Brudenells, with the mansion house called Chalfont House or the Old Place, a farm near it and the field around, and also Oakgrove farm (near the site of St. Mary's School).[63] Lady Mary's half-brother, Horace Walpole the writer, visited them there, soon after they arrived, in company with his architect friend, John Chute. 'Last week,' he writes, 'we were at my sister's at Chaffont* in Bucks., to see what we cold make of it: but it wants so much of everything, and would require so much more than an inventionary of £5,000, that we decided nothing, except that Mr Chute has designed the prettiest house in the world for them'. A.L. Rowse, in *The Early Churchills*, writes: 'Horace did not take much to this match to begin with, but he shortly became great friends with this gay, untidy couple, and remained on excellent terms with them all their long lives. They never had any money, but this did not cramp their good humour or their enjoyment of life. When Horace grew old, they were the faithful ones who did not fail to come and spend an evening with him. Lady Mary Churchill (as she was called in spite of her birth) was at length provided for by being made housekeeper in charge of Kensington Palace, and subsequently of Windsor Castle'.[64]

What they and Mr Chute did for the house can be seen from the

---

*'Chaffont' was the common pronunciation.

lower picture on page 24. It has suffered many alterations since, but we can still be grateful to them. Some of the work of Richard Bentley, another of Horace's architect friends, can yet be seen. Walpole wrote in 1760: 'I have returned from Chaffont ... Lady Mary is going to add to the number again. The house and grounds are still in the same dislocated condition: in short, they finish nothing but children: even Mr Bentley's Gothic stable, which I call Houyhnhnm Castle, is not rough-cast yet.' A description put out shortly before the property was sold in 1794, runs: 'The House is old, and though low is pleasantly situated: and, as well as the Estate belonging to it, was considerably enlarged by Mr Churchill, whose Taste also very much improved the Place, particularly in the judicious Disposition of the Water and the Grounds, and interspersing the latter with Plantations in a style of Elegant Simplicity.'[65]

The Duchess of Portland's Bulstrode

Let Horace Walpole lead us back to Bulstrode, where he was a welcome, if critical visitor: 'I have been often at Bulstrode from Chaffont, but I don't like it. It is Dutch and triste. The pictures you mention in the gallery would be curious if they knew one from another; but the names are lost, and they are only sure that they have so many pounds of ancestors in the lump.' 'The chapel,' he wrote, 'was formerly decorated with the assumption, or presumption, of Chancellor Jeffreys, to whom it belonged; but a very judicious fire hurried him somewhere else.' The Duchess gave him nine portraits of the court of Louis XIV: 'The Lord Portland brought them over, they hung in the nursery at Bulstrode, and the children amused themselves by shooting at them.'

The second Duke of Portland, and amiable person known to his friends as 'Sweet William', had married a rich and intelligent wife, Lady Margaret Cavendish Harley, daughter of the Earl of Oxford: and in her time Bulstrode became one of England's great houses. We have glimpses of the place and its life in letters of her friends (and what letter writers they were!) and especially in letters of her bluestocking friends, Mrs Elizabeth Montague and Mrs Mary Delany.[66]

The Duchess had the collecting mania: trees, flowers and fungi, birds, beasts and fishes, books, paintings, and miniatures, busts, coins and medals, shells rocks and fossils, 'English Insects and Exotic Insects' – she collected them all. (Not long before her death she 'collected' the famous Portland Vase now in the British Museum.) There is a pleasing description of a scurry round one day, to tidy away the books, papers and oddments that filled every chair, and then remove the comfortable chairs themselves, and 'set the blew damask chairs in prim form round the room', before the Princess Amelia arrived on a visit. Mrs Montague wrote: 'I believe the menagerie at Bulstrode is exceedingly worth seeing, for the Duchess of Portland is as eager on collecting animals as if where foresaw another Deluge, and was assembling every creature after its kind to preserve the species.' Mrs Delany says: 'Mr Lightfoot and botany go on as usual: Her Grace's breakfast room filled with sieves, pans, platters etc. on tables, windows and chairs.'[67]

The Rev. John Lightfoot, who combined the duties of curate at Uxbridge and domestic chaplain to the Duchess, deserves a special mention. He was one of the most distinguished naturalists of his time, a founder-member of the Linnean Society, and a Fellow of the Royal Society. His detailed notes give the precise localities of many plants in Buckinghamshire and neighbouring counties, which are in many cases the first written records. He gives the first description of the Reed Warbler; the nest and eggs were brought by a fisherman on the Uxbridge river to Her Grace. He gives accounts also of several new species of freshwater snails. Of one of them it is said that it was found on the leaves of a certain iris in water near Beaconsfield, by Mr Agnew, gardener to 'the Duchess of Portland, by whose sagacity all the preceding shells were discovered, and by whose faithful pencil they were drawn.' As to flowers, we have the evidence of an observant traveller, Mrs Lybbe Powys: 'The Duchess has every English plant in a separate garden by themselves' – a far remove from the formal gardens of earlier times.[68] As to the park, Mrs Delany is enthusiastic:

'Sunday after Chapel,' she wrote, 'the Duchess carried me a very pleasant airing she has had cut through a wood' [Dukes Wood] '3$\frac{1}{2}$ miles long, that joins to her park, and goes out on the common, which from a brown, dreary-looking heath she will by her bounty and good taste make very pleasant.' And later the same day: 'A pretty, uncommon scene is now before me on the lawn: a flock of sheep, shepherd and dog at a little distance, and in the foreground 15 or 16 hares, feeding with peacocks and guinea fowls.' And on a fine day in July, she writes that 'this place is like Paradise ... Such woods, groves, lawns and terrasses, not to be described and all enlivened by such a variety of creatures, in perfect agreement – beautiful deer, oxen, cows, sheep of all countrys, buffaloes, mouflons, horses, asses, all in their proper places. Then hares and squirrels at every step you take, so confident in their security that they hardly run away.'[69]

One of her letters begins: 'The Order in which the King and Queen and Royal Family with their attendants went from Windsor to breakfast with the Dowager Duchess of Portland at Bulstrode on Wednesday, 12 August 1778, the Prince of Wales's birthday.' In mock court style, she lists the procession, and reckons that, with 33 servants, there were 56 personages in all – 'a splendid sight as they drove through the park and round the court, up to the house'. Breakfast was served in the Long Gallery: 'The Royals walked through the great apartment, admired everything they saw, the young ones full of observation, and proper questions, some skipping, some whistling and delighted above measure, and charmed with the excellent breakfast, and ate abundantly.' Afterwards the Queen admired Mrs D's chenille work, and the King wanted to see her celebrated book of flowers, and fetched a chair for her. As she hesitated, 'Sit down, sit down', said the Queen, 'it is not everybody has a chair brought them by a King.' Mrs D ventured to remark that it had long been her wish to see *all* the Royal Family. 'You have not seen them all yet', said the Queen, 'but if you will come to Windsor Castle with the Duchess of Portland, you shall see them altogether.' The very next evening Mrs Delany was granted that happiness: first in the Queen's apartment at Windsor where the King and his seven sons came in to join the Queen and her five daughters; then, at a concert of music: and later, at a ball, 'begun by the Prince of Wales and the Bishop of Osnaburg dancing a minuet incomparably well'. (The latter was George III's second son, who had been appointed Bishop of Osnaburg in Hanover at the age of seven months.) It was midnight before Mrs Delany got back to Bulstrode, after a blissful day, not nearly as tired as she had expected to be.[70]

The Hunt

She also tells of a morning in November when she and the Duchess rode in a chaise 'to Gerrards Cross, about the middle of the common', for a meeting of the Royal Staghounds. The King and Queen arrived soon afterwards, with their retinue ('among them Lady Mary Forbes, who took three rooms at the Bull Inn, and breakfasted 38 people'). The stag was brought in a cart, and let out on the common.

Which reminds us of hunting as a local sport. It was not often that the Royal Staghounds met here (though as late as 1868 there was a memorable run via Denham, Pinner, and Wormwood Scrubs to Paddington Goods Station). But the foxhounds often met at Gerrards Cross. Indeed, there stood near the Packhorse until fairly recent times 'Huntsman's Hall', which was the kennels of the old Berkeley Hunt. An old account-book of the Hunt has an entry: '7 January – 20 March 1793. Thomas Oldaker's bills of wages, board and other expenses with the Whipers Inn, Helpers, Hounds and Horses at Gerrards Cross, £200 7s 4¼d'. Tom Oldaker, who built

Berkeley Cottage on East Common, was a famous huntsman of the times, who died in 1831 at the age of 80, and remembered a run when hounds finally lost a fox in the rough ground in Kensington Gardens.[71]

Gott of Newland

One local hunting enthusiast was Sir H.T. Gott of Newland Park. Newland had belonged for a hundred years to the Saunders, a branch of a well-known Bucks. family: but they did not prosper there, and the property came eventually into the hands of money-lenders, from whom it was bought in 1770 by Henry Thomas Gott. Gott's name was originally Greening, and he appears to have been the son of George II's head gardener. Already a man of substance, he inherited a huge estate from two ladies of the Gott family of Battle (Sussex) and adopted their name. He evidently laid himself out to be the country gentleman, rebuilding the house, redesigning the gardens, serving for many years on the committee of the Old Berkeley Hunt, as a Justice of the Peace, as Deputy Lieutenant of the county, and as Sheriff in 1774, when he was knighted. His wife had a Baronet-nephew who was for some time George III's Minister in Persia, and this interesting connection is remembered on a tablet in the church. Many pleasant stories have been told about the curious obelisk which now stands by the entrance to Chalfont Colony: but no doubt the simple explanation is that Gott had it erected to show the way to his Mansion at Newland.[72]

Bulstrode's Prime Minister

Mrs Delany reported, in 1776, a visit by 'the renowned Mr Burke': the ladies decided that 'take him out of politics, he is very entertaining'. But in the time of the third Duke of Portland, Edmund Burke, who lived at Beaconsfield, was often at Bulstrode, and no doubt more free to talk politics: for this Duke was much involved in the political fray for more than 40 years. Though not a brilliant man, he had a strong sense of public duty, and a gift for holding others together, and thus become in 1782–3 the head of the short lived Fox-North Coalition. But, like Burke, he hated the excesses of the French Revolution and feared its consequences here: and Bulstrode, which had been a great Whig House, became 'the headquarters of the Tory party'.[73] After Pitt's death, the Duke retired to Bulstrode; but he emerged again, reluctantly, in 1809 to become again Prime Minister for two harassed years before his death.[74]

In his time changes took place at Bulstrode. Humphrey Repton, the celebrated landscape gardener, was from 1802–5 employed upon the gardens and park, and found here a job after his own heart, 'under the direction of His Grace, whose good taste will not suffer any part of that beautiful park to be disguised by the misjudging taste of former times'. He comments that upon the great work 'are occasionally employed among the more efficient labourers a hundred children from ten to fifteen years old, who are thus early trained to habits of wholesome industry ... No object can be more delightful than the park scenery thus animated'. (One wonders about those children.)[75]

A year or two later, James Wyatt was commissioned to build a new house. Part of the south front was rebuilt, and a castellated Tudor-style wing took the place of the old west wing. But at this point the Duke's insecure finances caused work to slow down: £4,000 was owing to the architect, and soon building stopped altogether, not to be resumed until 1860. All that now remains of Wyatt's house is the isolated 'Pigeon Tower', once the garden entrance to the house.[76]

Overseers of the Poor

Dukes, Knights, and Squires: but what of the common people? The eighteenth century was not so good for them: some farmers prospered, some small traders went under, many labouring men were often on poor relief. Times were especially hard for poor families on the road, seeking work, but the accounts of the Overseers of the Poor (which contain some remarkable spellings) show how well on the whole, the village, at this time, looked after its own poor. Two Overseers were appointed by the Vestry year by year, and the job was no sinecure. There were regular monthly payments to be paid to those on relief, always some families who needed fuel or clothing, poor children to be apprenticed (and sent out properly clad), sick folk to be nursed at home or taken to hospitals in London. Several entries refer to the village 'cage' (which stood behind the church); and there is a payment in 1726 'for a new pare of stocks & oyorn work & Cullering them'. In 1741–2 there was a smallpox epidemic, and those afflicted were isolated in an infirmary or 'pesthouse' which stood by Austenwood Common. When another (less virulent) epidemic occurred in 1759 some were accommodated in the house of the windmill, which was near the pesthouse.

An Act of 1697 required anyone coming into a parish to bring with him a Settlement Certificate from his former parish. This bore hardly on many poor people, and cost the parish a great deal in time and money. A curious case was that of two men who worked for John Hatch at Chalfont Lodge farm. The parish boundary ran through the house; but after looking at a plan, the Justices decided that the men slept in Iver, and that Iver must be responsible for them.

The Village in the Eighteenth Century

Meanwhile the village was growing slowly: a few names and occupations may give a flavour of it:

Edward Ives, day labourer
John Russell, blacksmith
William Smith, currier
George Holder, waggoner
Henry Brown, cordwainer
William Nash, collar-maker
Thomas Hunt, maltster
Thomas Bradley, cooper
Henry Cooke, excise man
James Dakins, footsoldier
Thomas Price, miller
Andrew Burroughs, weaver
William Piner, brickmaker
John Bryant, sawyer
Edward Cawdery, carpenter[77]

Thomas Newman, glazier
Robert Hurles, thatcher
James Oakley, shoemaker
John Munke, barber and
    peruke maker
Robert Bennett, mercer
Henry Proud, higler
William Bonsey, tripeman
Richard Disborow, butcher
Thomas Dagger, tailor
Thomas Johnson, linen-draper
John Charsley, tobacconist
William Welling, sugarware
    potter

Besides these, of course, are the farmers, and an increasing number of victuallers. Thomas Piner, brickmaker, erected the Packhorse Inn and a smithy in 1708: and when the official Register began in 1753 there were (in addition to the inns already mentioned) the Kings Arms (kept by Henry Bennett), the George (Joseph Chitch), the Golden Ball (William Carter) and the Pheasant (then in Chalfont St. Peter). The Rose and Crown and the Waggon and Horses started life soon after this, and also the Fox and Hounds on the Oxford Road (now the Apple-Tree Restaurant). L.M. Wulcko in his pamphlet *Some Early Friendly Societies in Bucks.* mentions a Chalfont Friendly Society which was started at the White Hart in Chalfont St. Peter in 1795, and another begun at the Greyhound in 1806.[78]

Tradition says that 'Woodhill', by the 19th milestone on the Oxford road, was also for some time a posting inn. This house and its lands formed part of property given by the Duchess of Somerset to Brazenose College in 1679 (from which benefaction Somerset Iver Scholarships are still awarded). The house was largely rebuilt in the eighteenth century and is said to have contained a fine ceiling and staircase designed by the Adams brothers.[79]

The open-field system continued in Chalfont St. Peter until the nineteenth century (although Latchmoor Common Field was enclosed in 1847) and each year in the manor court it was decided which of the common fields should be sown, and which lie fallow. Throughout the eighteenth century successive Whitchurch Squires kept up their Manor Court in some style, appointing annually the constables, tithing-men, field-keepers and ale-tasters, and demanding headsilver from all their tenants. There are repeated injunctions to the landholders in Old Mead and Dewland Common to repair the ditches, banks, watercourses, stone bridges and ford: and several tenants are fined for removing soil from Gold Hill or bracken from Chalfont Heath. As the century goes on, incroachments upon 'Gerrards Cross Common' become more frequent, as new houses are erected: the original northern boundary of the common may be judged from that piece of it which adjoins the old school.[80]

Church records show that the number of families in the village of Chalfont St. Peter grew from 100 in 1705 to 160 in 1723. They included only two or three Quaker, and two or three Presbyterian, households. Our vicar at that time was also vicar of Bisley in Surrey, but he and his curate maintained services on Sundays, Festivals and four to six Holy Days, catechizing in Lent and Summer, and Holy Communion four times a year. The annual value of the living was increased by Queen Anne's Bounty to £46 18s 3¾d. 'The present vicar,' adds Mr Smart, 'takes 6d per house Easter offerings, not being able to get more, because the last vicar discontinued these for some years'.

The vicarage had been rebuilt in brick, and in 1707 was improved by the addition of 'a Necessary house, tiled and floored with deal, with two seats for men, and one for a child.[81]

Owing to the church's connection with St. John's College, and that college's connection with Merchant Taylor's School, several of our vicars had been educated at that school and afterwards gained high academic honours. For example, Mr Smart's successor, Moses Willes, was admitted to St. John's College from Merchant Taylor's in 1688, graduated in 1692, took his MA in 1696, and became Lecturer in Mathematics and a Fellow of the College in the following year. He then proceeded gently to BD in 1702, College Bursar in 1706, Vice-President in 1710, DD in 1711 and Dean of Divinity in 1712; and he remained a Fellow throughout his time at Chalfont St. Peter. However, it seems that these learned vicars and their curates carried out their necessary duties here; and one of them, at least, receives a glowing tribute on his memorial in the church – Dr John Chalmers, 'a faithful pastor of this parish for 28 years'. In his time the vicarage was again rebuilt, and he was given leave to make an entrance to it from the main road, in place of that from Vicarage Lane. From his time, also, are dated five of the church bells, cast by Mears of Whitechapel.[82]

An account of the Parish church's belongings in 1783 is simple, including two surplices, one Bible folio, two common prayers folio, three forms, and an umbrella. The Bible and the more handsome of the big prayer books, inscribed with a fierce Lion Rampant, were given in 1717 by Arthur Trevor, son and heir of Sir John Trevor, Jeffreys' cousin mentioned above.[83] The Account adds:

> Mr William Courtney, who died on December 5th, 1770, left an annuity of £400 stock in the four per cents, and the money arising from that annuity is to be dispos'd of in bread for ever for eleven poor unmarried women, eleven loaves one to each, and to the Clerk one, which are twelve to be given in the Church every Sunday after Divine Service. – Jho. Powell, Curate; Jn. Hunt, Jos Gurney, church wardens.

Mr William Courtney was a Rotherhithe maltster, who bought Tubbs Farm; perhaps he was a son of the Robert Courtney who was churchwarden of St. Peter's when the Rebuilding Appeal was sent out in 1709. His charity is still continued.

But a wind of change was blowing, that wind which found voice in Wesley and Whitfield. About 1772 Mr George Woodward obtained a licence for meetings for worship at the Mill House, Chalfont St. Peter, and a few years later he built a chapel beside Gold Hill Common; its pulpit was supplied for a time by ministers and students of Lady Huntingdon's Connexion and its first minister was a Mr Allen, who also kept a small school. A Meeting House on the present site was begun by Thomas Kean, and was opened in 1792, as an Independent Church. But in 1800 a Baptist became its minister; in 1807 it was recognised as a Baptist church, and as such it still flourishes. There was also a Nonconformist congregation meeting at Horn Hill, in the house of William Gillibrand, Overs Farm.[84]

Enter the Nineteenth Century

The turn of the century brought some notable changes amongst our gentry. In 1794 Chalfont Park was bought by Thomas Hibbert, in 1809 Thomas Allen bought Newlands, and in 1810 Bulstrode was sold to the Duke of Somerset. Mistress Ann, the last of the Whitchurches, died in 1809, and the Manor passed to her cousin, the Rev. William Jones of Chalfont St. Giles. The Hibberts, the Allens, the Somersets, and the Squire – these are our masters throughout most of the nineteenth century. In 1850 the Rev. William Jones was succeeded by his daughter Mary, wife of the Rev. Edward Moore; in 1885 Bulstrode passed to the Duke of Somerset's daughter Lady Helen Gwendolen, mother of Sir John F. Ramsden, Bart; in 1887 Chalfont Park was bought by Captain Penton.

Papers in the parish chest give some information concerning the village at this time. A Return demanded in 1831 shows that there were 180 inhabited houses, housing 686 males and 730 females. Of these, 149 were farm labourers, 28 men-servants, and 61 female servants. There were also two manufacturers – perhaps the two potters, one in Potkiln Lane, the other near Marsham Lane. Petty sessions were held every three weeks at the Pheasant, and the Constables appointed by the Court Leet had to report there. There, in 1856, Daniel Russell, who had the mill just above the Greyhound, appealed against his assessment. The mill had been used at various periods to produce silk, flour, and felt; Daniel was using it to grind flour, and had installed steam power.

The Overseers had paid Daniel Northcroft in 1825 for repairing the Church House and the Almshouses, and in 1836 for repairing the cage. But the Church House must have been demolished soon afterwards, for the site, the south-east corner of the churchyard, was levelled in 1849. 'The old dilapidated almshouses which adjoin the church yard' were removed in 1864.

The vicarage still had its farm buildings. In the church, James Cole in 1819 was employed to repair the old gallery, and John Clark was paid a shilling a week for playing the bassoon. There are regular payments of 'Ringing beer' to the bellringers; but in 1856 it was decided that their beer money on May 29th and November 5th should not be paid out of church rates.

'A Good Workhouse' and Bad Management

Village affairs, in the first half of the century, were in the hands of a clique, who appear to have been more zealous for their own interests than for the public good. This less pleasant aspect of village life is well illustrated by the story of the Workhouse, a story which has some significance in the grim history of Poor Relief.

In 1825 the Churchwardens and the Overseers of the Poor of the Parish bought three cottages on the west side of the village street, and built on the site a Workhouse (which still stands [1968], with its iron lamp-bracket). Ten years later (soon after Parliament had appointed Poor Law Commissioners) the experiment came to an ignominious end. The Inspector reported in no uncertain terms. The House, he said, was a good house, in very good repair: it could not easily be divided, but it would hold about 150 of one class, say, able-bodied men. At present, 'there are 35 in the house of all kinds, and amongst them two idiots'. 'This appears to be a very ill-conducted Parish: the Vestry is formed of small rate-payers and little shop-keepers. The Poor are farmed for £650 to the Master of the House, and the Overseer, who is a little Butcher, supplies the Master with the Meat for the House. This Overseer had made a very incomplete return, and on my giving him a return paper to fill up, both he and the Master of the house said that they could not tell how many Poor there were, but it was a well-conducted Parish, and they could get on very well without the assistance of the Commissioners. The Master of the house and the Butcher-Overseer clearly understood one another very well and, at the expense of the parish, did all they could to increase each other's gains. There was no attempt whatever to effect any classification – men, women, and children, sick and ill, and two lunatics, were all mixed together in the Chimney-corner. The Magistrates of this District, who are well acquainted with the state of this Parish, say that it is ill-conducted, that the jobbing is most infamous, and that of all the Parishes this most requires the interference of the Board'. In the following year, by Resolution of the Vestry, the Workhouse was sold.[85]

The Hibberts

The application for leave to dispose of the Workhouse was headed by J.N. Hibbert Esq. The Hibbert family has its memorials in St. Peter's Church, and its members deserve to be remembered in Chalfont St. Peter, to which they were notable benefactors. The family came from Marple (Cheshire) and had extensive interests in Jamaica.[86] John Nembhard Hibbert – of whom it is recorded that at the time of his death in 1885 he was one of the few survivors of those who had fought at the battle of Waterloo – gave land for allotment gardens, gave land for the extension of the churchyard, erected in the Amersham road 'buildings of plain Gothic architecture comprising an Infants school and two Almshouses, each with rustic porch' (pulled down in 1962): and also gave and endowed our invaluable Cottage Hospital, opened by the Lord Bishop of Oxford in 1871. After Mr Hibbert's death, the south porch of the church was erected as a memorial to him.

The Hibbert estate – 1037 acres – was broken up and sold in 1888. It included 'the Stately Mansion in Tudor style, with clock-tower and ivy clad turrets' (with the added attractions of 'capital wing – and ground-shooting, good trout – fishing in the Misbourne, and an Eel Weir at the lower end'): Chalfont Lodge (where some of the Hibberts lived); the Cottage Hospital; the Parish Room, formerly the Girls' School; Swan Farm and 155 acres, let to Mr

William Gurney of Chalfont St. Giles; Coldharbour and Oak End Farms; Isle of Wight Farm and 136 acres let to Richard and Edward Davis for £115 pa; the Mill House and 40 acres; the Watercress beds; Lambscroft Farm in School Lane (occupied by Mr Z. Lofty); and a meadow called Love's Delight (occupied by the vicar).[87]

New Tenants at Bulstrode

Bulstrode we left in an unfinished state, when the Portland money ran out. The Duke of Somerset, when he bought it, soon called in architects to finish the rebuilding: Robert Smirke was there in 1811, and Jeffery Wyattville soon after. But nothing came of it; instead, large quantities of building materials were sold. But part of the house was habitable, and was let to various tenants. It was taken in 1841 by Colonel George Alexander Reid and his two sisters, who liked it well enough to renew their lease seven years later, and to rent also Bulstrode Cottage in Hedgerley Lane (with the Little Park opposite), Pickerage House and farm at Fulmer, and Gerrards Cross Farm (Manor Lane).[88]

The Reids were children of Andrew Reid Esq. of Lyonsdown, Barnet, and Liquorpond Street, London, a Scot who was for many years a principal partner in one of the largest porter breweries in London. George, after leaving Oxford, entered the 2nd Life Guards, which he subsequently commanded as Colonel. Soon after his election, in 1845, as Member of Parliament for Windsor, he resigned from active duties, but continued as an unattached officer. He was a director of the London and South Western Railway in its early days, but chiefly devoted himself to his parliamentary duties, and was greatly respected in Windsor, to which borough he was a notable benefactor.[89]

They were not easy tenants. Miss Louisa wrote most of the letters to the Duke's Agent; and she pours out a gentle stream of complaints and requests – for new buildings at Pickerage, bay windows at Bulstrode, a new conservatory, and so forth. The Colonel had evidently taken on more land than he could well manage. In the late 1840s, the Duke's bailiff reports most of the farms tenantless, and only a man and boy at work in the gardens. Mr Allen of Moat Farm, gave up the struggle: 'All my efforts to reconcile that poor meek-hearted young man to the present depressed times are quite unavailing.' Miss Louisa would have taken on that farm also: 'The distress of the labouring class around Bulstrode through the want of employment suggested to my sister the idea of taking the farm to afford the opportunity of being useful to the Poor on the Duke's estate to advance this object she is willing to encounter the many difficulties of the undertaking in the inauspicious aspect of the times; but there must be a consideration from you to enable us to carry it out.' However, the Agent did not think the prospects of the farming interest so gloomy that the Duke should forego the modest rent. 'And so', wrote Miss Louisa, 'we must abandon the pleasure, and Mr Allen must seek a richer substitute ... But in this locality there are no fewer than ten farms asking for tenants! So much for the prosperity of Bucks![90]

It should be added that the Duke had the reputation of being an exceptionally good landlord. Conditions soon began to improve, and the Reids turned to other projects – cut short, alas, by the Colonel's unexpected death in 1852.

St. James

But now Gerrards Cross was beginning to emerge as a community, rather than merely a cross-roads. On August 30th, 1859, Samuel Wilberforce, Bishop of Oxford, consecrated the newly built church of St. James. The Duke of Somerset gave the land, which had been part of Fulmer Common, and the church was given by the Misses Anna Maria and Louisa Reid of Pickeridge, Fulmer, in memory of their brother, Major General George Reid, MP (N.B. The first vicar said in his first sermon: 'When the passing stranger inquires "Who taught that heaven-directed tower to rise?" you lisping babes shall articulate the names of your disinterested benefactors'.)

It was in 1856 that Miss Louisa, then living at Pickeridge, Fulmer, wrote to the Duke of Somerset's Agent, asking for a grant of Common Land for this purpose: 'We do not fear difficulties in carrying out our views as respects the Ecclesiastical arrangements, and Mr Tite's good taste and judgement would secure His Grace's manor from disfigurement.' The Agent, after consulting the Duke's lawyer, wrote:

'Maiden Bradley
7 May. 1856

'My Lord Duke,

I have been lately in correspondence with your Grace's lady tenants, the Misses Reid, of Pickerage Bulstrode, who have wished me to prefer their petition to your Grace that you will grant them a site on Fulmer Common for erecting a church at their *own entire expense*. Now at first it appeared quite startling, as having some serious question whether your Grace could make a valid conveyance of an *un*enclosed portion of the Common, though within one of your Manors; and therefore, not to trouble your Grace unnessarily, I applied to Mr Jennings for his opinion, who considers your Grace to have full power under the Church Buildings Act, 50 George III, and as the site – say, two acres – forms part of the Common, not of any actual value, it would decidedly be of advantage to your Property, as adding respectability in that locality.

A site had been offered them, by the Lord of the next Manor, but this seems more central, and meeting more general approval. It seems the contemplated Building is to be in commemoration of their Brother, the late General! I should really respectfully say, there could be no possible objection on your Grace's behalf, and it would be an everlasting and distinct confirmation of your Title to the Manor.

The Ladies seem anxious for as early a reply as your Grace could give.

I have the honour etc.
M.J. Festing'

The Duke replied promptly, readily acceding to the ladies' request; negotiations were set on foot, Mr Tite produced his design (reminiscent, it is said, of Pisa, to which the General had had a special attachment) and the building – carried out by Hardy & Sons of Cowley – was completed in 1858, although, owing to the law's delays and the Bishop's engagements, it could not be consecrated before August 1859. It was a notable act of faith, for there were few houses near it; but the church served some in other parishes who lived at a distance from their own parish church, and in 1859 'the Consolidated Chapelry of the Church of St. James, Gerrards Cross', was created by Order in Council, embracing parts of Chalfont St. Peter, Iver, Fulmer, Langley Marish and Upton-cum-Chalvey. The eminent architect Sir William Tite, MP, a friend of the Reids, certainly achieved something different from the usual run of Victorian Gothic. Experts of the time praised the originality and skill of his design: opinions concerning its appearance varied, then, as now.[91] The first vicar, the Rev. W.J. Bramley-Moore, son of John Bramley-Moore, Esq., MP of Langley Lodge, published a little book, *The First Sabbath at Gerrards Cross*, which contains the sermons preached on that first Sunday, a poem he had written about the church, an architectural description, and an 'Address to the founders of the New Church from the surroundings inhabitants', with a list of 300 of these inhabitants which includes many familiar local names. The first vicarage, we learn, was 'Latchmoor'. A fuller account of the building of the church and its subsequent growth is given in *Gerrards Cross and its Parish Church* by E. Clive Rouse and J. Gordon Harrison, published in the centenary year 1959.[92]

Schools

In J.J Sheahan's *History and Topography of Buckinghamshire*, following a description of Gerrards Cross as a 'highly respectable place consisting of many genteel residences and some cottages built on the verge of the extensive common ... nearly 1,000 acres, mostly covered with heather and furze', we read: 'Opposite to the church, a very neat building for a school, with residence for the teachers attached, is now (1861) in course of construction. The school building is in the form of a cross of equal length and breadth – measuring 32 feet each way exhibiting four gables.' The Rev. Edward Moore, of Stone Dean, Lord of the Manor of Chalfont St. Peter, gave the land for the school 'for the education of children and adults, or children only, of the labouring, manufacturing, and other poorer classes ... in the Principles of the Established Church'; and the school gained a grant from the National Society, other substantial subscribers being the vicar and the Duke of Somerset. The first teacher, who lived in the very small house adjoining the school, was Miss Jane James, who received £35 per annum, plus furnished house, fuel and light. After the 1870 Education Act, the number of scholars rose from 41 in 1870 to 93 in 1879. In that year Mr Charles E. Colston was appointed headmaster. He came straight from college and continued as head until his resignation in 1920 – a long and notable career, both in the life of the school and in the life of the village, for he took an active part in public life.

In *Gerrards Cross C.E. School 1862–1962*, compiled by the present (1968) headmaster, Mr Lewis J. Simpkin, are extracts grave and gay, from the School Log Book, which help one to realize how different life was then, when there were no cars or bicycles, and Gerrards Cross was a predominantly agricultural area. For example:

> 'February 1865: Re-admitted L.S. and G.L. who had stayed away during the winter on account of the weather: both under six years old.'
> 'July 1863: Very poor attendance. The older children help in haymaking and fruit picking.'

The history of Chalfont St. Peter school is longer and more complex. As we saw, there had been a school in the Church House in the seventeenth century: perhaps it continued, intermittently, until the nineteenth, for in 1843 there was a 'National School' on that site. Ten years later, that had been pulled down, and a new school for boys and girls erected in 'School' Lane (schoolmaster, Joseph Marfleet), as well as the Hibberts' Infants' school which was noticed earlier. Besides these, the Rev. David Ives, the Baptist minister, kept a boarding school at Gold Hill House, Mary Northcroft (next door) had a day school, and there were other private schools, varying from Dames' schools at 2d a week to superior establishments at 6d per week.

As numbers increased, the girls of the National School transferred, first to the lecture room in Churchfield Road (given by Mr Hibbert) and then to the Church Room (given by the Rev. G.M. Bullock). In 1892 Girls' and Infants' Schools were built on the present site, and in 1912 the boys moved from School Lane to an extension on the same site.[93]

Roads

The busy main street of Gerrards Cross, now full of cars, is named after the patient packhorse, and useful he must have been, throughout most of our history, when the roads were little more than cart tracks. The eighteenth century Turnpike Acts brought some improvement to the main roads, though as late as 1797 a traveller could report of the Oxford Road near Uxbridge that there was only one passable track on it, and that less than six feet wide, and eight inches deep in liquid mud. Not until the influence of the blessed Macadam spread in the 1930s was any substantial improvement made. Under the Turnpike Act of 1752, there was a toll-gate at Tatling End on the Oxford road: and, on the Wendover road toll-gates at Oak End and Gravel Hill. The Bull and the Greyhound were noted coaching inns. It is said that at the Greyhound the coaches changed to broader wheels, seeing that tolls on the way to London were based upon the width of the wheels. For the rest, there was the useful carrier: in 1853, John Hunt left Chalfont St. Peter early every Thursday morning for the Angel in Farrington Street, returning on the Saturday, whilst Thomas Shackell drove from Gerrards Cross to Clements Inn, Old Bailey. Until Gerrards Cross station opened in 1906, the nearest railway station was at Uxbridge, so that the carrier was much in demand. Gerrards Cross – what there was of it – then centred on the Bull, and the smithy and post office opposite, the little Post Office being a central office 'whence letter bags are dispatched to surrounding towns and villages'. The office was a small attachment to 'Flint Cottage' (demolished in 1962) where for over 90 years the Matthews family also carried on a tailoring business. The present Gerrards Cross Post Office was built in 1912.

Roads sometimes fade away; the main road from Chalfont St. Peter to Beaconsfield used to lie along Layters Lane, and thence by what is now only a cart-track called Mouse Lane to 'Wilton's Green', now enclosed in Wilton Park. An eighteenth-century owner of Wilton Park extended the park, diverting the Oxford Road, closing some lanes that ran through the park, and making that straight road from A40 to Jordans which is known as Potkiln Lane, from the old-established pottery there.[94]

Since the break-up of the old estates and the coming of the railway many new roads have been constructed; and the names of some of them happily perpetuate the old field names, such as Hither Meadow, Garners End, Foxdell Way, Winkers Close and Howards Wood.

Orchehill

One estate sold early in the twentieth century was that of Orchehill.[95] Orchehill House (now St. Mary's School) was the home of William Blount, who married Lady Charlotte, sister of the 12th Duke of Somerset. Their park extended from Marsham Lane to Claydons Lane, and one lodge may still be seen at the junction of South Park Drive and the Amersham Road. Another is still to be seen at the far end of Bulstrode Way, whence a drive, known as Lady Charlotte's Drive led across the fields and the Packhorse Road to Orchehill House. William Blount and Lady Charlotte are commemorated in the east window of St. James's Church.

The General

A notable figure in Chalfont St. Peter in the first half of the nineteenth century was Lieutenant General Terence O'Loghlin, a veteran of the Napoleonic wars, who had been wounded at Tournai in 1793, and subsequently commanded the Brigade of Guards under Wellington in the Peninsular War. He bought the Grange in 1802 and lived there until his death in 1843. He has his memorial tablet in the church, and also his vault, which he is said to have sampled not long before his death.[96]

Mayne Reid

Amongst the congregation at St. James in its early years might have been noticed a swarthy gentleman, with black imperial and mustachios, a dandy in his dress, with lemon kid gloves, who generally appeared to be more interested in the ladies' bonnetts than in the service. This was Mayne Reid,[97] adventurer, soldier, and writer of a large number of romances and boys' stories, once immensely popular. (Connoisseurs should sample *The White Gauntlet*, a romance which has its setting in this locality in ye olden times.) He had lived and fought in Mexico, and he built in 1866 beside the Oxford Road (near Huesden Way) a 'rancho' in the Mexican style. Unfortunately, further building speculations at Gerrards Cross involved him in heavy loss and in 1867 he returned to the United States.

The Colony

A notable newcomer was the National Society for Epileptics which in 1894 purchased Skippings Farm, with £4,000 given by J. Passmore Edwards, Esq. Tubbs Farm and Roberts Farm were added later, and the colony today consists of an estate of over 350 acres, including its own farm, orchard and market gardens, a self-contained community where 500 men and women are accommodated in 19 separate houses, and are trained, employed, and cared for.

The Twentieth Century

An elderly resident of Gerrards Cross who as a boy attended the school on the Common, recalls a day when the headmaster said: 'I have heard that a Motor Car is to come along the Oxford Road this afternoon: if you behave yourselves you may go across the Common, and watch it go by.' It was behind schedule, but before they saw it they could hear it chugging along the quiet road.

The motor car and the railway have brought great changes. George Stephenson had a scheme for a railway from London to Aylesbury, but it did not materialise, and it was not until 1904–6 that the Great Central and the Great Western jointly constructed the line through High Wycombe. In the Gerrards Cross section this involved building a high viaduct and digging a long and deep cutting, and the imported navvies who worked on the job are still remembered. They had their hut dwellings, their Navvies Mission, and their 300 pints waiting for them at the Packhorse when they knocked off. The contractors were Messrs. Paulings, and the station was opened in 1906.

The deep cutting complicated the main drainage scheme carried out in 1910–11. The surveyor stated then that the number of houses in Gerrards Cross had increased from 75 to 325 in four years, and he based his scheme on 500 more. The extensive development in recent years south of the Oxford Road does not seem to have been then contemplated.

Another change was a strange work of nature. In 1911 Gerrards Cross Common was on fire and burned for three months. Before that time it had been a wide open stretch of heather and gorse: afterwards the silver birches sprang up everywhere, and the common became a pleasant woodland, in which it is hard now to find a sprig of heather.[98]

The New Parish

The first Annual Meeting of Gerrards Cross Parish Council[99] was held on November 25th, 1895, when Colonel the Hon. W. Le

Poer Trench, CVO, RE, of St. Hubert's was elected chairman. The Ordnance Survey Department was asked to send two representatives to perambulate the bounds of the new parish. Mr Witham was appointed meersman on behalf of the parish, and the boundary posts were eventually put up ten years later. It was proposed to celebrate the coronation of King Edward VII by planting an avenue of trees across the common from the cross-roads to the Packhorse, subject to the consent of the Lord of the Manor and the copyholders (who had common rights): but the Lord of the Manor was far from enthusiastic, and no one could or would tell who the copyholders were. The emptying of cesspools was a continual headache, as the community grew, and in 1910 a Steam Motor Exhauster was purchased. But it was generally believed that sparks from this unlucky machine started that fire on the common, and it was sold again two years later. Chalfont St. Peter was asked to join in the main drainage scheme, but did not think that necessary. The arrival of the railway contractors caused some anxieties; additional Parish Constables were appointed, and the General Post Office was asked to supply a bicycle, to expedite the delivery of telegrams.

Even before the station was opened, development began: Marsham Way and Woodlands, Bulstrode Way and Orchehill Avenue were constructed. Chalfont St. Peter proposed a Joint Voluntary Fire Brigade, but Gerrards Cross did not think the time opportune. A serious fire occurred in Oak End Way in 1913, and another in Station Road in the following year. It was discovered that there were not enough hydrants, those there were could not be found; when they were found they were buried under some inches of road; when they were dug out the key was not available; when the key was found there was insufficient pressure of water. However, Uxbridge Fire Brigade was summoned, and arrived in less than an hour. In 1908 a proposal to obtain control of the common was put forward. The Parish Council worked at this for years, before in 1920, control was at last gained, and suitable bye-laws accepted. In that year, Chalfont St. Peter suggested that the two parishes might become one Urban District Council area, but Gerrards Cross did not think the time opportune. In 1912 a scheme for the administration of the Chalfonts and Gerrards Cross Cottage Hospital was amended by the Parish Council, in order to maintain the right of local doctors to attend their own patients in the hospital.

The Brighton of Buckinghamshire

It is interesting to turn the pages of directories and guidebooks of a few years ago. Gerrards Cross is called 'the Brighton of Bucks.',

Above: two wagons and locomotive under the long girder bridge carrying Mill Lane over the line, viewed from the East, with temporary rail lines; below: a steam navvie used to make the cutting through Gerrards Cross, with part of one of the waggons used to carry away the spoil just visible behind the horse.

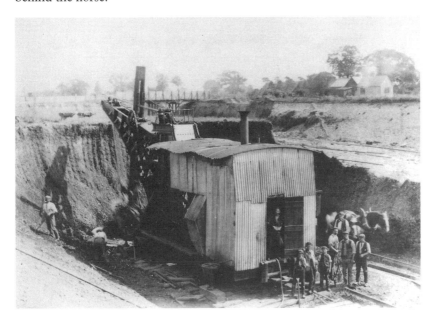

Above: the construction of the arches of the western viaduct crossing the A413 to Amersham; below: the competed eastern viaduct crossing the Misbourne River.

Above: view from Gerrards Cross station of the Packhorse Road bridge. At the time this photograph was taken the excavation of the cutting had not yet reached the required depth. Below: Latchmoor Estate, viewed from the metal railway bridge.

Latchmoor Estate, Gerrard's X from Railway Foot-Bridge.

Above: Gerrards Cross station – the 'down' line building in early stages of construction, with the Packhorse Road bridge in the distance; below: the station, viewed from the East, nearly completed.

Above: the first 'down' train from Marylebone at Gerrards Cross station, April 1906. Below: station staff on the 'up' platform at Gerrards Cross, 1919.

with reference to its health-giving quality, 300 feet up, with a deep gravel soil. 'The water from the village pump on Gerrards Cross Common was noted for its curative powers for those suffering from rheumatism, and people from distant places used to make a pilgrimage to drink it.'

In 1907, when the Latchmoor Estate was being developed, we are told: 'As for communication with London, the fact that Mr Sam Fay, JP, the general manager of the Great Central Railway is a resident of Gerrards Cross should be sufficient security on that score. The station is only 27 minutes from Paddington or Marylebone, and it is even said that the latter terminus will be attainable in 17 minutes when the new line is in complete working order.' A quarterly season ticket then cost £3 1s 0d 'but this will be considerably reduced, and the service improved, as the district develops'. 'The modern bugbear of rates and taxes can have no terrors in this parish, for the local rates are as low as anywhere in the kingdom, being only 4s 4d in the £'. 'The style of architecture of the residences is for the most part of that quaint domestic type so characteristic of Buckinghamshire ... For £650 upwards a splendid residence can be secured, standing in its own grounds.' Twenty years later, when land at £100 per acre is still obtainable, it is stated: 'It is one of the features of the district that all the good class property is grouped in one part and the artisan type in another part.'

Chalfont St. Peter was also developing rapidly. Soon after the coming of the railway, the Common Downs estate was opened up, on the former common field of that name; the Petersville estate, north of the village, followed in 1921; and not long afterwards the Swan farmland were sold for building, and became the Chalfont Heights estate. New building continues, especially in the Chalfont Common area. Now (in 1968) the by-pass road, planned many years ago, has recently been completed, and a new shopping centre in the village is being built. These developments, together with the creation of a car-park on the site of the old vicarage, have gone far to change the nature of the place. According to the 1968 figures, the population of Chalfont St. Peter was 13,980 of Gerrards Cross 6,257.

Developing Communities

As the villages grew, a host of social activities began to develop. The golf course in Chalfont Park was laid out in 1921; the Hockey Club (President, Sir John Ramsden, Bart, of Bulstrode) also played in the park, where the big house was now a residential hotel. Gerrards Cross Cricket Club (President, Colonel Le Poer Trench) played on the common, opposite the Bull; the Chalfont St. Peter Cricket Club, in Newland Park. Their President was H.A. Harben, Esq. of Newland, who was Chairman of the Prudential, one of the pioneers of industrial assurance, and a generous benefactor to the village, who gave the hall at Horn Hill. The miniature Rifle Club had its outdoor range on land belonging to Sir Sam Fay of Raylands Mead. The Gerrards Cross and Chalfont St. Peter Fire Brigade had been formed in 1914, as the result of a public meeting called by Mr C.P. Lovell, after that serious fire in Station Road. 'Since the sale and conversion of the Town Hall into a garage,* the amusements of Gerrards Cross have become entirely centred in the Oak End Hall and Assembly Rooms centred in Oak End Waye.' Gerrards Cross at this time had no 'Picture Palace', but there was one at Chalfont St. Peter.

In Chalfont St. Peter, St. Pauls Chapel-of-Ease at Horn Hill had been built in 1866. In 1914, All Saints Church in Oval Way was consecrated, and in the following year, St. Joseph's Catholic Church by Austenwood Common (rebuilt and enlarged in 1962). A Methodist Church was opened in Oak End Way in 1912 (and a new church built on the same site in 1960) and the Congregational Church in Packhorse Road was opened in 1922, the Hall being added eight years later.

The names of those who gave their lives in two World Wars are commemorated on War Memorials in the two villages. After the first war, a memorial scheme was put forward in Gerrards Cross for the purchase of the vicarage (formerly 'Watercroft') and grounds of nearly three acres, for a Social Centre: but it was not until after the 1939–45 War that this was accomplished. The house (since extended) is now the home of the active Community Association, and in the entrance-hall a plaque bears these words:

In loyalty to the memory of those who gave their lives in the war of 1939–45, this Centre is dedicated to the fostering and furtherance in good fellowship of all arts and exercises healthful and enriching to body and mind, to the end that by the grace of Almighty God we, the living may together cultivate in the spirit of true community, the national heritage preserved for us and for our children at so great and sacred a cost.

In Chalfont St. Peter, a Memorial Hall was built at the lower end of Gold Hill Lane. This was demolished, when the dream that some had long kept in mind was realised by the building, in 1962, of a fine new Community Centre, with hall, canteen, and smaller rooms, on the playing fields north of the village; and this is now in full use.

*In Station Road.

With so large an increase in population, the Chalfont St. Peter Primary School, under its headmaster, Mr S.H. Bagley,[100] needed to increase its accommodation, and a new school also was opened in 1963 in the Chalfont Common area. A Secondary Modern School, 'Old Jobs', was opened in 1947 and under the direction of Mr G.F. Horley has advanced both in quantity and quality; in 1961 the first part of its new buildings in Narcot Lane was opened, designed by the Country Architect, Mr F.B. Pooley. Numerous private schools also flourish, and Gerrards Cross' long-promised new Primary School has (in 1968) recently been completed.

Newcomers, who are unaware when they pass out of Chalfont St. Peter into Gerrards Cross, are sometimes puzzled by the parochialism of the two villages, which is accentuated by the fact that Chalfont St. Peter belongs to one rural district (Amersham) and Gerrards Cross to another (Eton). Proposals to amalgamate the two villages have been talked of for years.

'Newland' is now a teachers' training college, 'Chalfont Park', research laboratories, and 'Bulstrode' the home of the World Evangelisation Crusade. In the village, modern shops and multiple stores have arrived, and some light industries have their works. With the tentacles of London reaching out ever further, and the volume of motor traffic ever increasing, local councils have struggled valiantly at times both to provide more housing and also to preserve something of the village character of Chalfont St. Peter and Gerrards Cross, surrounded, as they are, by 'green belt' land; and this struggle continues.

THE HISTORY OF BULSTRODE

A.M. Baker PhD, FSA

Above: a modern aerial view of Bulstrode, courtesy of WEC International.
Below: St. James's Church, Gerrards Cross. Photo: Barbara Lyddiatt.

1

Early Times

Until the coming of the railway in 1906, Bulstrode was far more important than its near neighbour Gerrards Cross. In pre-Roman days it was a centre of population and of defence. In the Roman period a pottery industry grew up, while in the Middle Ages it developed into a considerable estate owned by the Bulstrode family. It was, however, in the eighteenth and nineteenth centuries that Bulstrode became a celebrated centre of political and cultural life.

Bulstrode Park is now a pleasant open space to the north-west of Gerrards Cross and is almost entirely enclosed by a brick wall. It is difficult to imagine how the area looked in pre-Roman times when there were no roads, hedges or other artificial divisions and when human settlements were separated only by rivers, forest and scrub. The land was marshy, and a river very probably ran along the dry valley which runs roughly from north to south. Bulstrode and the land which ultimately became Gerrards Cross formed a single plateau which falls away on all sides to river valleys: the Thames, the humble Misbourne and Alder.[1] In ancient times the inhabitants probably lived along the banks of these rivers. The earliest were the people of the Old Stone Age whose tools and weapons were made of flint; there then followed a time known as the Mesolithic Age, and this developed into the New Stone Age when the tools were beautifully shaped and worked. There is plenty of flint in this area, and a factory for making flint implements was discovered in the Misbourne near the railway viaduct over the A413.[2]

By about 1200 BC bronze was introduced and then, six hundred years later, iron. These metals were valuable and at first were used mainly for armour for the chiefs. Magnificently decorated shields and helmets have been discovered, but generally the armour was buried with its owner. Meanwhile, flint and deer's antlers were used for ordinary purposes. Few tools of any kind have been found in or near Bulstrode.

It was probably during the mid Iron Age that Bulstrode camp was constructed. It forms one of a chain of great hill forts which guarded the chalk escarpment of the Chilterns and which were placed at intervals of about ten miles. The fort is difficult to date because so few finds of implements or pottery have been made there, but Mrs Stainton, who is an authority on this period, suggests that it is contemporary with the even grander fort on Ivinghoe Beacon which, from pottery and other finds, can be dated

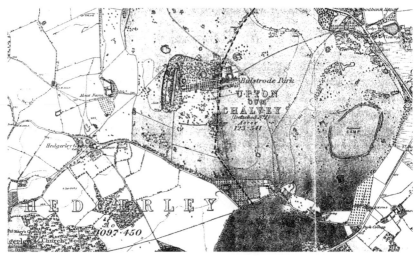

6 inch to 1 mile Ordnance Survey map showing parish boundaries and camp, surveyed in 1864-76.

to about 400 BC. The hill forts may be associated with the crosses of Whiteleaf and Bledlow. These would have been simple vertical scars in the chalk and may have been phallic and thus associated with fertility cults.

It used to be thought that hill-top forts were dwellings of chieftains, but they are now considered to have been 'camps of refuge' to which the tribes living in the area could withdraw in times of danger, taking their flocks and herds with them. In times of peace the forts were probably used as places where crops and other valuables could be stored.[3]

Bulstrode fort occupies a flat area of about 26 acres. It is surrounded by ramparts and ditches; the ramparts are about six feet above ground level and the ditches about six feet deep. These are double round most of the perimeter, but single where the hillside is steep. It has a fine entry gate on the north-east corner, and another, almost opposite, which leads to Windsor Road. It is amazing to think of this colossal work being accomplished with tools of flint or antler horn. The enterprise must have entailed great organisation and involved a very large number of people. The camp has never been systematically excavated. A small dig took place in 1924 sponsored by Sir John Ramsden and supervised by Sir Cyril Fox and other eminent archaeologists, but only one hearth was found.[4] The whole of the level area was ploughed during the 1939-45 war, but few surface finds were made. Then in 1968 a main drainage trench was dug, which crossed the rampart at the north-east gateway. This work was very carefully supervised, but again no

90

finds were made. Near the edge of the trench, possible 'post-holes' were discovered which may have been connected with a timber building. Large timber buildings were erected in the Iron Age, and a splendid circular example has been built in the Chiltern Museum near Chalfont St. Giles. People who have gardens encroaching on the ramparts are forbidden to dump rubbish in the ditches or to put in poles or to plant trees.

The only evidence of Roman occupation in the Bulstrode area is a series of pottery kilns. The first of these was discovered near Wapseys Wood in 1935. Two of them were nearly complete. They were of the 'up-draught' type with a clay-lined combustion chamber where the pots were fired. A tunnel linking the kilns to the stoking pit was uncovered. The fuel was oak, beech and hazel. The products of the kiln included dishes, bowls, cups and beakers. In 1963 the sites of three more kilns and stoking pits were found. More recently yet, another kiln was discovered in a garden in Hedgerley Lane. Pottery made at the Wapsey's Wood kiln has been found on the sites of the splendid Roman villas which were built in other parts of Bucks. The pottery is rough in texture and greyish in colour; examples can be seen in the Aylesbury Museum.[5]

The Romans made a preliminary expedition to Britain in 43 BC, but began to settle about one hundred years later. Their rule lasted nearly four hundred years (i.e. about the same length of time as between the present time and the death of Queen Elizabeth I). During the Roman period sizeable towns developed, and fine villas such as Fishbourne grew up in the countryside. In Bucks it is

Rampart of the camp.

estimated that the villas were spaced at intervals of about ten miles. The finest of those in Bucks is Latimer.[6]

In the fourth century barbarians began raiding the peaceful Roman provinces, and the great Roman empire began to crumble. The chief enemies of the British were the Angles and Saxons whose homeland was the inhospitable sand banks and marshes of Denmark. Britain was almost undefended. In vain the people called on Rome to send soldiers to help them, but their entreaties were ignored.[7] In 410, when Rome itself was attacked, the final blow fell and the last legions were withdrawn from Britain.

There is not a great deal of physical evidence of Anglo-Saxon settlements in South Bucks. The settlers usually lived in huts grouped round a fine decorated hall which was the dwelling of the chief. A good picture of their lives can be gleaned from heroic poems such as *Beowulf*. Their presence in the Bucks area can be deduced from place names; the ending -*ham* means settlement (e.g. Denham, Amersham and Chesham) and *ings* means clearing in a wood, as in Innings and Skipping above Chalfont St. Giles. (Chalfont is an older name from *Cheadles Funta*, derived from *Cheadle* a British surname and *funta* meaning a spring.[8])

In time the Anglo-Saxons were converted to Christianity and developed a highly sophisticated culture; the craftsmen were pre-eminent in sculpture and illumination, and the writers in composing wonderful poetry. They made progress in the organization of social life, especially at local level, and prepared the way for the introduction of fully-fledged feudalism. According to this system all the land belonged to the king; he granted large areas to his chief followers and supporters, who came to be known as *tenants-in-chief*. In return these important people vowed loyalty to him and promised to bring a specified number of armed men to help him if he went to war. In turn, the tenants-in-chief granted or, as was said, 'enfeofed' their own followers with parts of their own estates. These smaller holdings were called manors. The more important of the sub-tenants had to promise to follow their lord if he went to fight in the king's wars, while the others, who were basically peasants and were called villeins or bordars, undertook the actual cultivation of the land. The overlord reserved a part of the land for his own use, and this was called the *demesne*. The rest was farmed communally. There were large open fields for growing crops in which each member of the community was allocated strips. There was also 'waste' where they could graze their cattle and meadowland for hay. Swine could be fed in the woods. In return these peasants had to work for specified hours on the demesne and had to perform certain duties.[9]

Some fifteen years after the Conquest, William decided to order a great survey, partly to make sure that he was receiving all the rents which were due to him, and partly so that he would know who was holding the land and who had held it in the time of Edward the Confessor. The chronicler says that William 'wore his crown at Gloucester', i.e. held a council of his adherents, and ordered that a great inquiry should be made. 'So closely', continues the chronicler, 'was the survey made that not one yard of land, nor one ox, nor one cow nor one swine was left out that was not set down in the record.' The survey was made by royal officials who asked who now held the land and what it was worth; how much the overlord held in *demesne* (i.e. for his private use) and how much was worked by the villeins and bordars.[10]

The unit for land measurement was called the 'hide'. This usually comprised the amount of land that could be ploughed by one team of oxen in one day, multiplied by 120. (This was the area which was considered to be enough to support one family.) In modern terms it was about 120 acres.

Bucks is fortunate in having very complete Domesday entries for each manor. There are often several manors in a modern parish, but these merged in the succeeding years, and the parish became an ecclesiastical unit.

Bulstrode was not originally a manor on its own; parts of it were in Hedgerley, which was itself included in the great manor of Eton, and parts were in Farnham Royal, Chalfont St. Peter and, most importantly, in Upton. The connection with Upton was maintained into the nineteenth century. A map of 1878 shows the parish boundary actually running through the middle of Bulstrode house. A slate in the wall of the lane running along the south boundary of the park has arrows which point to Hedgerley in one direction and Upton in the other. There are two manors in Upton, both of which were held by King Harold before the Conquest. The larger one was assessed at eighteen hides, of which land for ten ploughs was held in demesne. There were nineteen villeins with five bordars with fifteen ploughs, and there were two serfs. There was a mill worth four shillings and fisheries for 1,000 eels. There was enough meadow for two ploughs and woodland to feed 200 swine. Altogether it paid 21 pounds. After the Conquest it was granted to Hugh de Bello Campo.

The overlord of the smaller manor was William Peverel, an important tenant-in-chief whose estates were based in Nottingham. He enfeofed an undertenant called Robert [surname unknown]; according to Domesday he held three hides; there was land for five ploughs on the demesne; there were eight villeins with three bordars who had three ploughs (about 400 acres). This is about the area of Bulstrode Park in the nineteenth century, and it is here suggested that this second Upton manor developed into the park.[11]

It is not unusual for manors to include detached portions. Other local examples are Beaconsfield, which was part of Burnham, and Penn which was part of Taplow. It has been suggested that the main parts of the manors were low-lying and subject to flooding so that the overlords tried to get possession of drier land for pasturing their cattle in winter. (This may not be the case at Upton as both manors seem to have included just enough land to pasture their ox teams and meadowland to make hay for them in winter.)[12]

It is at this time, when Anglo-Saxon overlords were being dispossessed in favour of Normans, that the legend of Bulstrode is set. The story is first found pasted into the cover of a book of letters written by Sir Richard Bulstrode who died in 1711. It tells how a Norman lord who was a follower of William the Conqueror was granted land in this area which belonged to an Anglo-Saxon overlord called Shobbington. Shobbington, determined to resist, called out his tenants and servants, who were very numerous. He was helped by his neighbours, the Penns and Hampdens and their followers. William sent a thousand of his troops to help the Norman lord. The Anglo-Saxons 'cast up works' which, as the author says, 'remain to this day'. The Normans camped outside these entrenchments, but the Shobbingtons 'managed a parcel of bulls' and, sallying out of their entrenchments by night, surprised the Normans. Many of the Normans were killed and others fled. William himself did not dare attack such resolute enemies, so he sent a herald and promised Shobbington a safe conduct to court. Shobbington agreed and rode to meet William on a bull. After some negotiations, Shobbington promised to swear allegiance to William if he was allowed to keep his ancestral estates. The family then took the name of Shobbington-Bulstrode, but Shobbington was dropped. The author goes on to say that the truth of the story is witnessed by the survival of the entrenchments and also by the crest of their arms which is a 'bull's head cabossed'. Shabbington (derived from Shobbington) is the name of a village near Thame. The arms of the family of Shobbington are quartered with those of Bulstrodes in the fifteenth and sixteenth centuries.[13]

2

The Bulstrode Family and the Brasses in
Upton Church

It is interesting to trace the rise of the Bulstrodes, not only because
of its importance in the history of this area, but also because, in a
wider context, it is typical of the way in which the lesser gentry rose
to wealth and influence during the Middle Ages and the early
Tudor period.

The early history of the family is difficult to elucidate. In 1950
Henry W. Bulstrode compiled a chronological account of the
members of the family, which he called *The Book of Bulstrode*.[1]
There is a MS copy in the Library of the Bucks Archaeological
Society, and there are other, fuller versions in the British Library
and the Library of the Genealogical Society.

The first part of the history is highly conjectural, as it depends
largely on the repetition of Christian names. The author traces the
pedigree back to a Geoffrey of Northants who was living at the time
of the Conquest. He had two sons, one of whom stayed in
Northants and took the name Burcote, while the other came to
Bucks and was known as Barstrode. The family likes to connect this
name with the legend of Bulstrode, but the Place Name Society has
a more factual explanation and considers that the name is derived
from Saxon words *Bur* or *Buhr*, a fort, and *Strode*, a marsh, referring
to the Iron Age camp overlooking the valley which is dry now but
which was probably wet and marshy in earlier times.[2]

The verifiable history of the family begins in the twelfth century.
The author was able to consult Pipe Rolls, Close Rolls and charters
as well as wills and local records, and one of the first mentions of
the family is in 1170, and in 1185-6 Radulfo and his son Nicholas
Bulstrode witnessed a charter in the cartulary of Missenden
Abbey.[3]

There are several mentions of Bulstrodes in the thirteenth
century. Adam, a clerk, became a prebendary of Southwell in 1272,[4]
but other members of the family seem to have been turbulent and
law-breakers; Sampson de Bulstrode, for instance, was put in prison
for causing the death of Johanne, wife of William Draiton.[5] It is
significant that a marriage between John Bulstrode and Agnes
Shobbington is recorded in 1265.

At about the time that the Bulstrodes were establishing themselves in Upton, they were acquiring land and influence in the

neighbouring manor of Chalfont St. Peter with which it had a common boundary and which is within an easy day's ride.

The Domesday entry for this manor is very detailed. Like Upton it had been a royal manor before the Conquest, having belonged to King Harold's brother, Leofwine, who was also killed at the battle of Hastings. King William confiscated the manor and granted it to his half brother, the bishop Odo of Bayeux (who was probably responsible for the famous tapestry). Odo granted part of the manor to Roger d'Anquetel, one of his followers. He himself then rebelled against the king and was banished, and all his estates were forfeited. William gave the Chalfont manor, among Odo's other possessions, to the de Montfords, Dukes of Leicester, whose descendant, Simon, is held to have founded Parliament. The history of the manor of Chalfont St. Peter is very complicated and can be studied elsewhere.[6]

The name Montford is commemorated in the name of a farm called Mumfords overlooking the Oxford Road which became the manor house. The name Montford occurs frequently in the area in the Middle Ages. In the twelfth and thirteenth centuries, the leading family was the de Turvilles; there were two brothers, Richard and

12th century wall painting in the Chapelle des Templiers, Cressac sur Charente a Templar chantry.

Robert. They were very pious, and Richard, who died in 1226, made valuable grants to religious foundations. The first of these was the grant of the church of Chalfont St. Peter,[7] which he rebuilt, together with the rights of presentation, to the newly founded Abbey of Missenden. His second gift was of a stretch of land, with pasture, arable and a valuable mill to the house or preceptory of the Knights Templar that was established on the boundary of the manor of Hedgerley. This land is called Turvillesland or Temple Mead, and lay where the Community Centre now stands. The Knights Templar were a fraternity of knights, vowed to poverty and chastity, whose aim was to protect the Christian Kingdom of Jerusalem from infidels. The order was supported by a series of farms or preceptories founded throughout Christendom by benefactors and became very rich.

There is no charter for the foundation of the preceptory at Hedgerley. The first mention of it is in 1190 when Henry de Pinkini, Lord of Fulmer, gave permission for the community to pasture three hundred sheep on Fulmer common (probably Dukes Wood). The preceptors were not always above reproach, for in 1276 the preceptor of the house was accused of taking a bribe to let a robber go free.[8]

In 1308 the English King Edward II dissolved the order in England, probably because he was jealous of their wealth. In 1324 the Pope dissolved the order completely; curious stories were circulated about the Knights, and they were accused of practising Black Magic and of worshipping idols. (This is part of the story of the Turin shroud.)[9]

When Edward II confiscated the lands of the Templars at Hedgerley the estate remained in the King's Hand (i.e. administered by royal officials for a short time), and then was granted to the Knights Hospitallers, a somewhat similar order. The Hospitallers failed to take up the grant and in 1328 they transferred it to Hugh le Despencer, the hated favourite of the King.[10] When Hugh fell from favour the estate was transferred to the Abbess of Burnham, on condition that she paid £15 a year for the maintenance of Hugh's widow. While the estate was in the King's Hand, it was administered by a royal official called William Turk who left an inventory of its assets.[11]

The Bulstrodes were also active in Chalfont St. Peter. Mr Bennell points out that by the early fourteenth century the original manor of Chalfont St. Peter had been divided into three. The first was the original manor, and the second was an estate called Champions or Campions which occupied a site in the area now known as Chalfont Park; the third part was Turvillesland which, as already shown, was granted by Richard de Turville to the Knights Templar at Hedgerley. About 1320 Geoffrey established himself in Champions (the name is derived from the name of the original owner, Hugh le Champion, to whom it belonged). A family called Goys succeeded le Champion in this estate, and it was through them that Geoffrey acquired it.[12]

The estate adjoined Turvillesland which included arable and meadow lands and a very valuable mill on the Misbourne. Geoffrey decided to try to absorb it. During the time of confusion in the affairs of the preceptory at Hedgerley, Geoffrey seems to have received a royal grant of the estate; this was contested by the Abbess, and a long lawsuit ensued. Geoffrey became impatient and decided to take direct action; it is recorded that he, his brother John, with John Cok of Burnham, William atte Garston, Ralph Haywood and others 'broke the house of the Abbess, the spindle and iron of her mill, and her hedges there, cut her corn and moved and consumed her grass and dispastured it with cattle and carried away the trees'. She complained that no-one would now work for her. It is not surprising that the king issued an order to impress Geoffrey for 'forming bands to murder, rob and commit other offences in Bucks and Middlesex'. In spite of this condemnation, Geoffrey was still in possession in 1361, as is witnessed by the fact that he owed the service of two knights' fees to the king's son for it.[13]

Geoffrey was himself a man of substance and had other manors in different parts of England. He was Keeper of the Manors of Fordingham in Dorset and Adridley in Shropshire; he kept his interest in Dorset for, even while he was engaged with his struggle against the Abbess, he became MP for Dorchester.

Geoffrey had several sons, one of whom continued his father's violent ways, for he was implicated in an assault on Thomas Cheynduyt. His oldest son John, however, opted for a quieter life, for in 1345 he was apprenticed to Thomas de Wurlingworth, goldsmith. He qualified by about 1380, for John of Gaunt's register records that John Bulstrode of London supplied a cup of silver for a present to Phillipe de Mohun on the day of his marriage. In another document John is called *orfeau* and was freed from being put on an assign and from being made mayor or sheriff. He was evidently a citizen of London and an important man, for in 1419 the famous mayor, Richard Whitynton, assumed guardianship of his daughter. John was buried in the church of Old St Paul's before the high cross where the gospel was preached. After his death he is referred to as late citizen of London and goldsmith. There is no evidence that he lived in either Upton or Chalfont.[14]

It is difficult to trace the history of the family in the fourteenth and fifteenth centuries because Christian names are repeated in several generations and also because people at this date had very large families.

It is clear that the Bulstrodes absorbed a number of other manors. First, as already shown, Geoffrey managed to keep possession of

Turvillesland in Chalfont St. Peter. Second, Thomas Bulstrode gained the manor and the manorial rights of Upton. An inquisition of 1350 refers to a tenement called Bulstrodes tenement for service to the king of a quarter of a knight's fee.[15] (This implies he was a tenant-in-chief.)

During the period of the fourteenth, fifteenth, sixteenth and seventeenth centuries, members of the family were increasingly drawn into employment by the court and great lords. The first recorded appointment of this kind was that of Edmond, the brother of Geoffrey who married Maud the daughter of Henry Duke of Lancaster and became valet to his father-in-law. Later, in 1346, he was given the office of notary to the diocese of Lincoln. In return for his services he received many manors which were distributed all over the country. Among the assets which he himself had inherited was an oven.[16]

Richard Bulstrode, the son of William of Upton, who died in 1503, was appointed Keeper of the Great Wardrobe to Margaret wife of Henry VI and had been Comptroller to the Household to Edward IV. Richard's eldest son, Edward, continued the tradition of public service; at the foot of his commemorative brass in Upton church there was a brass plate, now lost, asking those who saw it to pray for him, and he described himself as 'Esquire to the body of King Henry VII and King Henry VIII'. It is known that he made the arrangements for the funeral of Henry VIII and that he attended Henry VIII at the Field of the Cloth of Gold when he went to meet King Francis I of France – a gorgeous occasion! He died in 1517. His heir was George who married Joan Piggot, one of whose daughters became Maid of Honour to Queen Katherine of Aragon, Henry VIII's first wife.[17]

The history of the family in the late fifteenth, sixteenth and seventeenth centuries can be traced through a study of the brasses in the Upton church. This church is one of the most interesting in Buckinghamshire. It may originate from the eleventh century, but its main features are characteristic of the twelfth century.[18] It originally consisted of a narrow nave, a ringing chamber under a central tower, and probably a small chancel which was destroyed after the Conquest. It had belonged to King Harold, but William the Conqueror confiscated both the manor and the church with its emoluments and granted them to one of his followers, Hugh de Bello Campo (Beauchamp). His son, Pagan, granted them to the Augustinian canons of Merton in Surrey.[19] It is not certain whether he granted the manor as well. The canons used the chancel as their own chapel, rebuilt it in a richer style and excluded the laity. It consists of two bays which are divided by semi-circular responds and an unmoulded transverse arch; the ribs are rolls on a flat unmoulded band and they rest on corbels. The ribs were decorated

Above: church interior showing chancel. Below: nineteenth-century south aisle, church interior showing brasses mounted under the arches.

with a simple geometric pattern painted in black, red and yellow.[20] This was accidentally destroyed in 1841 while the church was remodelled, but was immediately restored.[21]

The chapel was used exclusively by the canons, and was cut off from the nave by a wall pierced by a small round-headed arch which led into the ringing chamber under the tower. Side altars on the east wall of the nave were used by the laiety. When the monasteries were dissolved by Henry VIII in 1538, the chancel was opened up for use by the laiety, but the division seems to have remained. Important residents of the area, such as the Bulstrodes, who wished to commemorate their forebears, began burying them under great slabs of stone let into the floor on which memorial brasses were mounted. These brasses consisted of portraits of the man, his wife and children, accompanied by shields bearing their coats of arms.

In the nineteenth century the church was nearly derelict. The tower had been struck by lightning and the rest of the building was in ruins. It was nearly demolished, but at the last minute benefactors came forward who not only repaired the existing building but also enlarged it by adding a new aisle on the south. In order to give access to this from the old nave, they broke through the south wall and replaced it with an arcade of pointed arches resting on fat circular Norman-style pillars.[22] The architect was Benjamin Ferry, a pupil of Pugin who was the architect of many small churches and also rebuilt Bulstrode House.[23]

At Upton, Ferry carefully preserved the vaulted chancel, but he took down the wall with its small round-headed arch which separated it from the nave. He also took down the two pointed arches which probably sheltered the nave-altars on either side of the opening into the tower chamber. Eventually the three arches were built into the east wall of the new south aisle which he added to the church. This is recorded in the nineteenth-century *Records of Bucks* and is confirmed by the author of the South Buckinghamshire volume published by the Royal Commission on Historical Monuments.[24] The older round-headed arch forms a recess in the middle of the wall and the pointed arches are placed on either side. These are of different sizes and date. The one nearest the chancel frames a beautiful wooden carved arch with shafts and capitals which may have come from one of the side altars; these were used by the laiety, while the high altar in the chancel was monopolized by the canons. The central arch probably dates from the twelfth century, and the other two are thirteen or fourteenth century. The one near the window has a continuously moulded jamb.

The Bulstrode brasses are now erected vertically within the second and third recesses. (The re-erection of the brasses in this way is controversial. No doubt they suffer less from wear and tear and are more easily visible, but it would be more correct to see them

Illustration of brass of Agnes Bulstrode who died in 1462. Inscription figures of children now lost.

in their original positions.) Unfortunately, when this work was carried out at Upton, several figures were lost and also inscriptions and coats of arms.

The earliest of the Bulstrode brasses is a female figure who is kneeling and clad in a shroud.[25] She is now placed at the top of the central arch, over the figures of Edward Bulstrode and Cecill Croke. This figure represents Agnes Bulstrode who died in 1462; she was wife of William Bulstrode who died ten years later. The antiquarian Browne Willis recorded the figure of Agnes and the inscription in 1733.[26] When members of the Bucks Architectural & Archaeological Society visited Upton in 1891, Mr Russell reported that a rubbing had been made of this brass in 1829 and that this had shown the figure of Agnes and the indent for the figure of William, together with his shield.[27] He said that the rubbing had been given to the Archaeological Institute.[28] This has been identified by Mr McHardy as a rubbing in possession of the Society of Antiquaries of London. The rubbing shows the figure of Agnes and on smaller plates the nine sons and two daughters of the couple. The daughters wear butterfly head-dresses which were in fashion during the second half of the fifteenth century. It also shows the one surviving shield, and the inscription:

Orate pro animabus Willi Bulstrode & Agnetis uxoris ejus filie Willi Norreys de Bray et pro animabus Rici Roberti Isabella Johis Willi Edmundi, Agnetis Thome Rogeri Henrici et Georgii filior[em] pi dei Willi Bulstrode et Agnetis que quidem Agnes mater obijt 12° Die Aprilis A° [anno] Dni [domine] MCCCC LXII et Anno Regis Edwardi quarti 11° et praedictus Williis Pater Anno ... aetatis ... [not filled in]

Browne Willis also gives a diagram of the arms on the one surviving shield which shows Bulstrode quartered with Shobbington. As the charges are included in all the shields associated with the Bulstrodes, they are given here:

Bulstrode
sa stags head cabossed arg attired or, between the antlers a cross patty fitchy of the last, through the nostrils fess-way an arrow or feathered arg, i.e. on the black ground a stag's head cut off at the neck; between the antlers a cross with the bottom arm longer than the others and all expanding towards the extremities; through the nostrils crossways a gold arrow feathered with silver.

Shobbington
argent a chevron gu between three squirrelss syant sa up and eating nuts, i.e. on a silver ground a red chevron between three squirrels sitting up eating nuts (nuts probably red).

This William, who is known as William of Upton, was a very important figure in the history of the family. It is interesting that Agnes was portrayed dressed in a shroud for this mirrors the preoccupation with death so characteristic of the late Middle Ages.

Next in date to the broken memorial to William and Agnes is that commemorating Edward Bulstrode (d. 1517) and his wives; this occupies the whole of the space within the recess on the east wall of the south aisle nearest the window. A book containing rubbings of shields which accompanied monumental brasses, including those of

Memorial breass to Edward Bulstrode, d. 1517, and three wives; from Lack, *et al* (1994). One of the wives and the inscription is now missing.

Upton, is also in the Library of the Society of Antiquaries. These were probably made in the mid-nineteenth century. The rubbings are accompanied by exquisitely written notes which help to identify the charges. Unfortunately these brasses were already badly defaced when the rubbings were made. It is strange that, while the monumental figures are excellently preserved, the shields were almost indecipherable even in the mid-nineteenth century.

Edward stands in the centre and figures of two of his three successive wives stand on his left, but sadly that of his first wife, Mary Empson, which stood on his right, has disappeared. Shields on which the arms of Edward himself and the three wives are placed in the corners of the recess. In the illustration in the book by Lack *et al.*[29] all three wives are shown; it must therefore have been taken from an earlier rubbing. There are several rubbings in the library of the Society of Antiquaries which show all the figures, and the illustration in the book is evidently based on one of these.

Lipscomb gives an excellent description of the figures and the costume. He says that Edward's hair was cut short and combed down on either side of his face and that he wore plate armour with a skirt and gorget of ringed mail. It can be seen that the hilt of his dagger is below his right elbow and that his sword, which hangs from his reticulated belt, has a pyriform pommel. He continues by describing Edward's broad-toed shoes and his large spur rowels. He also describes the ladies. Mary Empson, his first wife, wore a square

Photograph of arms: Bulstrode quartered Empson (Edward's first wife; brass missing).

head-dress with long lappets of embroidery and had sleeves with deep ermine cuffs; round her waist was a long girdle passing through a rosette and hanging to the ground; this ended in a tassel or jewel. The other two ladies looked towards their husband and were placed more in profile so that the backs of their head-dresses were visible. Otherwise their costume was like that of Mary Empson, but there were no jewels at the end of their girdles. Below the figures there was a rectangular plate, now lost, which bore an inscription:[30]

Of your charite pray for the Soules of Edward Bulstrode Esquire for the Body of King Henry 7 and Kyng Henry the 8th, and Mary, Helen & Margaret his Wyffes; which Edward deceased the 2° day of August in the Yere of our Lord God MVXVII, on whose Soules Jhu [Jesus] have mercy.

The shields in this recess at Upton bear charges which relate them to Edward and his wives. They are now erected in the corners framing the figures. As already shown, it is very difficult to decipher the charges. The shield which relates to Edward is now placed in the bottom southern corner under the wives (in the book by Lack *et al.* it is shown in the top northern corner; it is not known why it was moved, but perhaps this was its previous position).[31]

The charges are Bulstrode 1 and 4, Shobbington 2, but 3 is complicated because the arms of Kniffe are included on 2. Richard Bulstrode married Alice Kniffe in 1503. The arms of Bulstrode and Shobbington are the same as on the brass of William and Agnes. Those of Kniffe are placed at the top of the shield, i.e. in a chief, in a separate compartment or canton. They read: *sa paly of six arg and az two knives or swords in saltire blades arg, hilts or*, i.e. on a background with six silver and blue stripes there are two knives or swords crossed diagonally the blades are silver and the hilts gold. Below the canton there are other charges which seem to be five small open roses or perhaps *mullets*. These arms have not been identified.

The shields of the three wives are all divided vertically (i.e. per pale), the charges of Bulstrode, Shobbington and Kniffe being on the dexter side and that of the wife on the sinister. The shield belonging to Edward's first wife, Mary Empson, is now placed in the top north corner of the recess. The colour of the background (field) is not known. The charges are a green chevron between three small gold bags tied at the neck. In the notes accompanying the rubbing in the Library of the Society of Antiquaries these are called *filiastres*, but in Burke's *General Armoury* they are identified as *bougets*. These are objects carried on a pole, rather like a yoke.

The shield bearing the arms of the second wife, Elyn Brant or

Brent, is placed in the bottom northern corner of the recess. The sinister part of the field, which belonged to Elyn, bears the arms gules *a wyvern arg rampant*, i.e. on a red ground a silver beast (rather like a griffin) standing on its hind legs in a threatening position.

The shield bearing the arms of the third wife, Margaret Norrys, is placed in the top southern corner of the recess. As usual, the arms of Bulstrode, Kniffe and Shobbington are on the dexter half and those of Margaret on the sinister. These show *a bend arg three cinquefoil flowers*, i.e. on a wide silver band running diagonally there are three open five-petalled flowers. Margaret outlived her husband and was buried at Hedgerley where the family had property.

On the memorial the children of the wives are shown in small scale under the brasses commemorating their mothers. Mary Empson had four boys, Elyn Brant seven boys and two girls, but Margaret Norrys had ten children; a brass on which she and the children are commemorated is in Hedgerley church. This must have been brought from the original church which was not on the same site.

The finest of the Bulstrode brasses is that commemorating Edward Bulstrode and his wife Cecill. Edward died in 1599; he was the son of Thomas and grandson of Edward who died in 1517. Cecill was the daughter of John Croke who held the manor of Chilton, also in Bucks. Like Edward, John was a prominent lawyer.[32] The brass occupies the lower part of the central recess under the figure of Agnes Bulstrode and a small rectangular plate which bears a Hebrew inscription reading 'I know that my Redeemer liveth.'

The figures of the numerous children of the couple are shown below the main figures, and there is a most beautifully lettered inscription written in English which reads:

Here lyeth bvried the bodye of Edwarde Bulstrode Esqvier, and Cecill his wife, one of y davghters of Iohn Croke Esqvier, by whome he had issve .4. sonnes, Henrye, Thomas, Edward and William and .vj. davghters, Elizabeth, Margaret, Anne, Cecill, Magdalen, and Dorothy. Whoe departed this mortall Life y last daye of Avgvst in the yere of our Lorde God. 1599

There is also a small plate bearing the name of the first wife of Henry (Edward's eldest surviving son). This has now been moved to the west end of the south aisle.

Although Edward and Cecill were Puritans, they wear the most elaborate clothes. Again, Lipscomb described them; he says, Edward 'has no helmet and his hair is short; he has a thin pointed beard and whiskers on his upper lip. Over his armour he wears an

Memorial to Edward Bulstrode (d. 1599) and his wife Cecill Croke, from a rubbing in the library of the Society of Antiquaries of London (shields and scrolls now missing). From Lack *et al* (1994).

embroidered or embossed doublet with long flaps apparently made of overlapping steel plates.' These plates, which have pleated leather or velvet edging called *picadills*, prevented the flap rubbing on the graves which cover his legs. He has a long sword with a large hilt and round pommels. The armour contrasts strangely with the sleeves of his doublet which have scalloped wrist-bands and the great pleated ruff which surrounds his throat. Cecill wears a similar ruff. On her head she has a low-winged headdress without lappets but partly covered by a veil. She has a pleated stomacher cut short at the waist which is partly covered by her gown; this hangs open to show her embroidered or damasked petticoat whose hem is decorated with a wreath.[33]

These figures were not intended to be seen in isolation. A fine life-sized rubbing in possession of the Society of Antiquaries shows them as part of a large composition which, like the other Bulstrode brasses, was embedded in the floor of the chancel. Above the heads of the figures were three shields bearing the coats of arms of Edward and Cecill;[34] highly decorative three-dimensional scrolls with verse inscriptions floated upwards from their faces and over the heads of the figures. Between these was a small plate bearing a Hebrew inscription which, in translation, reads 'I know that my Redeemer liveth.' (This is now mounted below the figure of Agnes Bulstrode.)

Browne Willis recorded the inscriptions which cannot be read on the rubbing. They are difficult to understand, so I asked my cousin, Paul Winby, for assistance; he enlisted the help of a Latinist friend. Both inscriptions refer to the death of Edward and Cecill. The Latin on Edward's scroll reads: *Fleres si scives unum tua tempora mensi* (You would weep if you knew the end of your days), and that on Cecill's: *Rides cum sit forsitan una Dies* (You would smile if perhaps it happened on the same day).

The rubbing of the brass which is included in Lack *et al.*'s book is taken from the big rubbing belonging to the Society of Antiquaries, but it is less impressive on a smaller scale. In spite of Cecill's protestations, she married again after the death of Edward.

It is now difficult to interpret the shields above the heads of the figures, but Lipscomb made rubbings of them in 1824, which are now in the Library of the Buckinghamshire Archaeological Society in Aylesbury. The shield over Edward's head shows the Bulstrode arms, that above Cecill's head the Croke arms, and the central shield is Bulstrode quartered with Croke. Both Browne Willis and Lipscomb list the charges on the shields.

The last of the Bulstrode memorials in Upton church commemorates Henry Bulstrode, the eldest surviving son of Edward and Cecill. He died in 1643. He married twice; his first wife was Maria, daughter of Thomas Reed of Barton near Abingdon, and his second wife Bridgetta was the widow of John Allen, citizen of London. Henry was

(b)

(a)

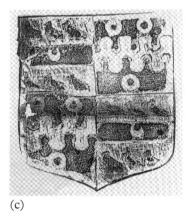

(c)

Rubbings of shields over the figures of Edward and Cecill, made by Lipscomb in 1824. (Library of Buckinghamshire Archaeological Society, Alyesbury). (a) from shield in centre. (b) shield over head of Edward Bulstrode. (c) shield over head of Cecill Croke: Croke quartered Bulstrode.

an important man; he entered Oxford when he was thirteen and then joined the Inner Temple. The family had interests in Cornwall as well as Bucks, and Henry was MP for Helston in 1614 and then for Bucks in 1625; later he was appointed Sheriff of Bucks. He was very wealthy. In 1626 he nearly doubled his property by buying the estates of William Drury of Chalfont St. Peter. (The Drurys had acquired the manor and considerable property in Chalfont when Missenden Abbey, which had owned it, was dissolved.)[35]

It seems probable that Henry rebuilt Bulstrode House, which is said to have burnt down during the reign of Elizabeth. It is interesting to find that the old engraving of the house by Bowles

110

shows details which are consistent with the architectural fashions of the early seventeenth century.[36]

During the Civil War Henry took an active part in the fighting. He raised troops to protect the Hampdens who were being persecuted by the King, Charles I. It seems likely that he, the Hampdens and other Buckinghamshire Puritan gentry drilled on the camp in Bulstrode Park. This no doubt contributed to his financial ruin.[37]

Lipscomb records that the monument to Henry was in the nave. Browne Willis records the inscription. The monument was in the form of a tomb chest with a flat top. This was broken and was apparently lying about in the churchyard. It is said the have borne indents of the figures of Henry and Bridgetta and of a shield with their arms.[38]

Only the front of the chest is preserved and is erected at the west end of the south aisle of the church. It consists of a beautiful rectangle of black polished marble framed with swags of white alabaster. On it there are two long inscriptions, finely cut; the first records the death of Henry and Bridgetta with particulars of their families. Bridgetta died in 1651.

Hic intumulatur Henricus Bulstrode filius primogenitus Edwardi B. & Cecilie uxoris ejus et Bridgetta fidelis uxor dicti Henrici antia Relicta Johis Allen civis Londiniensis, quae Bridgetta fuit filia Henrici Evans et Janae Uxoris ejus filia Johis Wake de Clevedon in Com. Somerset. A. et desponsata fuit dicto Henrico B. 20° Die Julij 1615, et placide dormivit in Christo 29 Octobris 1631. Et praedictus Henricus obijt in spe Resurrectionis ad vitam aeternum per Jesum Christum clementissimum Salvatorem suam.

The date of Henry's death is not filled in, but it occurred in 1643. The second inscription is in verse and refers to Bridgetta. It was transcribed by Browne Willis but unfortunately his writing is not always clear. The inscription was also transcribed by Lipscomb, and the readings are not identical; Browne Willis is the more accurate. A study of the inscription *in situ* shows that the wording is:

Invicta pietate necis prostrato trophais
Hec jacet hec oculos clausit utraque manu
Dulce mori aeterna anhelans terrestre reliquis
Mors mihi fit lucrum Christus et alma quies

The sense seems to be: 'she did not stain or throw away the unconquered piety of her upbringing; in sweet death she did not pant or strain for earthly advantage; death to me is the eternal light of Christ and perfect quietness.'

There is a small shield, again framed in alabaster, above the

Above: inscription detail. Below: detail of arms from the tomb of Henry Bulstrode, d. 1643.

monument; this is in good repair and retains its tinctures, but it is too high up to study. Browne Willis recorded the charges, but Lipscomb did not.[39]

As already shown, the Bulstrodes had accumulated large estates by grants, purchase and judicious marriages. In 1626 Henry managed to double these estates by buying up the possessions of William Drury who had taken over the assets of Missenden Abbey after it was dissolved in 1538. The Drurys had been wealthy and powerful. The purchases made by Henry included Chalfont Manor, the church with its assets, including the advowson, and also the Whapelode chantry in the church, the manor of Brudenells (originally Champions which had been owned in the fourteenth century by Geoffrey, now Chalfont Park) and Turvillesland and also Hedgerley Manor which Robert Drury had acquired by marriage. All this cost £13,000. Henry seemed confident and prosperous and could undoubtedly afford to rebuild the great house of Hedgerley Bulstrode which had been burnt down. Unfortunately he was overtaken by events.

During the first half of the century, tension between King Charles I and Parliament was growing in intensity. Mutterings of the disputes between the monarchy and the Commons can be traced to the end of the reign of Elizabeth, but the trouble came to a head during the reign of Charles I. Disputes became so acute that Charles dissolved Parliament in 1629 and only recalled it in April 1640 when there was an acute financial crisis occasioned by his efforts to impose the Prayer Book on the Calvinist Scots. This new Parliament brought up many grievances and was dissolved after three weeks. It is therefore known as the Short Parliament. The crisis became even more acute, and Charles had to call another Parliament in November of the same year which continued in session until 1653. The Commons forced many concessions on the King, but matters came to a head when he tried unsuccessfully to arrest five members who had taken the lead in opposition to him. Panic ensued, and the King withdrew to York where he was joined by his supporters.[40]

The Commons stayed in London where Puritanism was strong and where authorities called out the trained bands, the only well trained force in England. John Hampden was one of the threatened members and, partly in order to protect him, landowners in the Thames Valley and the Chilterns raised forces, drilled them and put the area in a state of defence. One of these landowners was Henry. It may be that his followers and those of his neighbours were drilled on the Bulstrode Camp. (Details of the legend of Bulstrode suggest that the old story about Shobbington and his neighbours may have been based on these activities.)[41]

There was much local activity, for the area lay across the route from London to Oxford where the King had now established his headquarters in 1642. Aylesbury was an important position across the route to the north. Henry took charge of this town and defended it against attacks by Prince Rupert. His bravery was commended but he was now nearly 60 and he died in 1643 while serving. He was succeeded by his eldest son Thomas who was appointed to a regular commission in Cromwell's army and was known as Colonel Thomas; he continued in the service until the end of the war. When he came back to Bulstrode he found that he had no longer the resources to pay his debts and run the estate. In 1648 he had to raise money by selling nearly all the assets amassed by the family during the last two hundred years. He said sadly the he was selling the 'inheritance of his ancestors'.[42]

The monument to Henry seems to be the last of those to members of the Bulstrode family in the church; it is said that his son, Thomas, was also buried here, but his grave has not been found. He had a very large family. It is clear that the Bulstrodes were still important in the nineteenth century and had a 'high seat' in the church, but it was destroyed in 1887.[43]

3

The Houses

(1) Hedgerley Bulstrode

Little is known about the original house. A villa was mentioned in 1265[1] and a Bulstrode Tenement in 1350, but it is not known exactly where these buildings stood.[2] The only definite information is that it was 'emparked' in 1552. This meant enclosing an area with walls, hedges or fences in order to prevent deer from straying or escaping during the hunt. This must have been carried out by Thomas, or more probably by Edward and Cecill Bulstrode. Many of the lesser gentry emparked their lands in imitation of the nobility.[3]

Legend tells that the mediaeval house was burnt down in Elizabethan times and, as suggested above, it must have been rebuilt by Edward and Cecill or their son Henry in the late

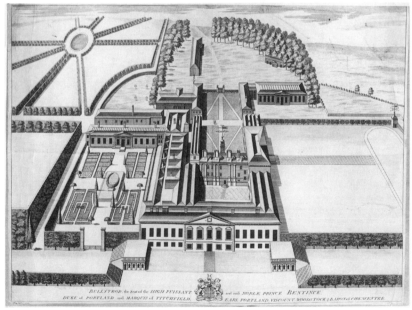

Bird's-eye view of Bulstrode House, an engraving by Bowles, 1730 showing Jeffreys' façades enclosing the remains of the old house.

Part of Judge Jeffreys' house which remained standing until recently.

sixteenth or early seventeenth century. Nothing of this house survives but there is an engraving by Bowles dated 1730[4] which looks down on the interior of the house behind the facades built in the 1680s by Judge Jeffreys. This engraving shows that there was a great courtyard divided transversely by a building whose exterior is ornamented by paired ionic pilasters and surmounted by a cupola.

In style this building is consistent with the rather clumsy classicism of English architecture of the late sixteenth and early seventeenth centuries. The courtyard in front of this hall is surrounded by buildings, but only their roofs are visible in the engravings. The only part of these which can definitely be identified is in the south-west corner where the chapel was located. It is certain that this was built before 1637 for, in that year, Archbishop Laud instituted an enquiry into private chapels. The report says, 'There is a loft round about it above to look into it through lattice windows'.[5] This chapel may have remained until 1865 when the whole building was demolished. It clearly remained unaltered in the eighteenth century, for in a letter of 1783 Miss Hamilton described how the Portlands 'met in the gallery, prayers were said and we went down into the body of the chapel to the pew next the altar to receive communion.' This was also described in 1783 by Mrs Delany.[6]

Turning again to the engraving, the long building on the south side which then faced into the courtyard probably housed a gallery, for Horace Walpole writing in the 1750s mentions a 'brave gallery of old pictures'.

The buildings on the east and west sides of the courtyard may perhaps have ended in towers at the north end, beyond the hall. The main entrance must always have been on the east side but this is difficult to see in the engraving. There is no evidence about the use of buildings on the west side next to the chapel. The courtyard north of the hall seems to have remained open. It has symmetrical paths, with a foot entrance on the north. Evidence survives about the exterior appearance of the buildings, for they are enclosed by the facades built by Judge Jeffreys.

As already shown, Hedgerley Bulstrode was sold by Colonel Thomas Bulstrode in 1645. It was bought first by the Gowers and later by Ambrose Bennett who died soon after, and then in 1675 by Judge Jeffreys.[7]

Judge Jeffreys is always regarded as a bogey-man because of the ruthless way in which he condemned to death ignorant peasants who had been induced to follow the Duke of Monmouth in his rebellion against King James II and the Catholic succession. Actually he was a convivial Welshman. He first came to this area through his cousins, the Trevors, who had bought the Grange in

Chalfont St. Peter. This was now a country house but had previously been the headquarters of the abbots of Missenden who administered the church and manor of Chalfont St. Peter. The Trevors, like Jeffreys, were prominent lawyers. No doubt Jeffreys saw advantages in living comparatively near London so, in 1675 when Ambrose Bennett died, he bought the estate of Hedgerley Bulstrode from his widow and nephew and immediately set about repairing it.

Mr Edmonds gives interesting details of the materials used for this work including £45 worth of bricks and 67 foot of Dutch tiles; while the work was in progress Jeffreys used the 'lettell house at Jarrats Cross'. This was perhaps the first authoritative mention of Gerrards Cross; the house was probably Raylands Mead which stood at the junction of Bull Lane and the present A40. The house, as it existed until recently, was a pleasant Regency building but the back parts were brick and one of the owners said that it had associations with Jeffreys and in fact his ghost used to walk!

The repairs to Bulstrode house at this time cannot have been very extensive for, after two years Charles II and some of his Court drove over from Windsor and dined with him. The King was affable and made Jeffreys sit down with him and drank to him seven times.[8]

Jeffreys' promotion was rapid, and he became Lord Chief Justice and then Chancellor. It seems that in about 1685 there was a serious fire at Bulstrode. Most of the house was destroyed but the old hall and chapel seem to have been saved. He now began a more complete rebuilding, living with his Trevor cousins at the Grange while the work went on. In 1676 the Manor of Temple Bulstrode was put up for sale by the Hills of Denham who had bought it from the Drurys. Jeffreys bought it and thus united the two Bulstrode manors.

Apparently the main house was finished when the cartographer Fisher was employed in 1687 to make a map of the estate. This is very valuable in showing the extent, layout and names of the various fields and closes, and details like the position of ponds, roads and footpaths. There is a long heading to the map which says that it shows parts of two manors – to wit 'the Manor of Temple Bulstrode and the Manor of Fulmer ... the principle [sic] House being commonly called or known by the name of Temple Bulstrode and situate in the parish of Upton'. This is misleading but it shows that Fisher and probably Jeffreys himself were attracted by the romantic connection with the Knights Templar.

This splendid map is now in the Aylesbury Record Office. At the top of the map there are small water-colour drawings which show elevations of the south and east fronts. The south front is very long and low and has a rather insignificant pediment in the middle. The windows on the first floor are tall and rather narrow. This is exaggerated in the five windows of the pediment. The windows on the ground floor are smaller and squarer. This reflects the arrangement of the interior, for the upper floor accommodated a long gallery while the bedrooms were on the ground floor. The gallery was very long. It impressed contemporaries who said that the comet which was then visible had a 'tail as long as the gallery at Bulstrode'. Behind this there were smaller rooms which communicated with it and may have also given access to the gallery of the old house, which housed the family portraits.

The east end of the famous long gallery in the front seems to have been divided from the rest to form a drawing-room. An idea of the appearance of these grand apartments can be obtained from Mrs Delaney's letter describing the visit of the 'royals' on the occasion of the birthday of the Prince of Wales.

The second drawing in the Fisher map shows the east front with the main entrance under a pediment in the middle. This looks higher than the pediment on the south front as the flanking buildings are of only one storey. The main doorway seems to have simple round-headed arches. There was an entrance hall from which a main stairway rose. Mr John Harris gave me a plan of the interior. Unfortunately it is not very clear; apparently there was a jumble of service rooms opening out of this hall. The hall may have been richly decorated as one of the ladies who was staying in the house refers to 'the gilded roof'.

Both elevations were built of brick, with stone quoins at the corners. The window frames were also of stone. Variety is also given by the stone string course dividing the upper from the lower floor and the white medallions under the roof.

Horace Walpole never liked the house. In a letter of about 1755, he wrote that local residents hated it because the red brick looked as if it had been dyed in blood. This is a reference to the reputation Judge Jeffreys had of excessive cruelty. The criticism of the brick is hardly fair, for one small part of the building which survived until a comparatively recent time (see p. 116) was built of the soft pinkish brick with burnt headers which is the typical material used in this part of Bucks during the seventeenth century. Walpole uttered his dislike of Bulstrode in other letters, calling it a 'melancholy monument of Dutch magnificence', and also that it was 'triste and sad'.[10]

Jeffreys did not enjoy his magnificent house for long, for James II, who was Roman Catholic and wished at least to secure toleration for his co-religionists, was driven from the throne and in 1688 the Protestant William of Orange and his wife Mary, a Protestant daughter of James, became monarchs. Jeffreys decided to take refuge overseas. He managed to board a ship at Wapping, but unfortunately he landed in order to have a last drink at a public house called the Red Cow and was captured and taken to the Tower of London where he died.

Apart from minor alterations, the house remained much the same and provided the setting for the brilliant cultural and social life lived there in the eighteenth century.

(2) Temple Bulstrode

Until recently little was known about this estate and its building. There was a lane called Temple Lane which led out of Hedgerley Lane. A little further afield there is Templewood Lane, the wood probably being part of the grounds. The field immediately in front of the present farm, called Moat Farm, had many humps and depressions in its surface, so there seemed enough evidence to warrant an excavation. This was undertaken by the Hedgerley Society and the Chalfont St. Peter and Gerrards Cross History Society in 1971. No trace of the buildings, which were erected in the late twelfth century, was found.[11] The main discovery was two brick and mortar floors which probably dated from the fourteenth century. Perhaps the most interesting part of the site is the moat which now runs behind the seventeenth century barns (hence the name Moat Farm). The structure of the moat was investigated without result, and an aerial survey was made which showed that the moat once extended across several other fields. Unfortunately, the whole area has been devastated by gravel digging".

There is, however, interesting documentary evidence about this farm or preceptory. As shown above, when the king dissolved the order of Knights Templar in 1308, it was administered by royal officials until it was regranted to the Knights Hospitallers and then to the Abbey of Burnham. While it was 'in the King's Hand' an inventory was made by William Molesworth, sheriff of Bucks, for the use of the Exchequer.[12]

There is further documentary evidence about Temple Bulstrode, for when the manor called Temple Bulstrode was sold in 1670 the description given was the 'Grange house, where William Meredew (bailiff) lately dwelt, on the site of the late great mansion house or manor house with outbuildings, a pigeon house, a four-acre garden plot and moat also Templefield and other closes abutting on it'.[13] This is clearly Moat Farm and identifies the site with that of the original preceptory. The fact that it is described as the grange house suggests that, before the Reformation, it was the headquarters from which the abbot of Bisham administered the estate.

The moat at Moat Farm.

Part of the moat and seventeenth century barns.

Excavation of the preceptory of the Knights Templar.

4

Bulstrode in the Eighteenth Century

After the disgrace of Jeffreys, his son and daughter remained in possession of the park and estate of Hedgerley Bulstrode for four years and then sold it to Hans William Bentinck, one of the closest friends of the new King William III. Bentinck had nursed William through smallpox and had probably saved his life at the Battle of the Boyne. Bentinck was a very cultured man and had been the Dutch ambassador to Paris where he had mixed in high society. Like all his family he was passionately interested in gardening.[1] English politicians who had brought King William to England were jealous of his Dutch advisors, so Bentinck began to play a less important part in government and he devoted himself to Bulstrode. He employed Talman as his architect and George London as his chief garden designer, but he also brought Dutchmen over to help.[2]

Bentinck did not alter the Jeffreys' house very much; with Talman's help he added pavilions and long raised terraces to each end of the south front and built an orangery at the back. The garden was laid out most elaborately, as can be seen in the second of the engravings by Bowles, a copy of which now hangs in the entrance of the house. Henry Wise who was in charge of the royal gardens may have helped also.

There was an enclosed garden at the east, apparently with a pavilion in the middle, and four rectangular beds laid out symmetrically round it. These were probably outlined and divided by low box hedges in the Dutch style. Behind this enclosed garden there is a large area with a pond in the middle and apparently tree-lined paths leading from it like spikes from a wheel; remains of this can still be traced.

To the north of this there is a straight canal of considerable length, a very Dutch feature. This is known as the Long Water and still exists, but is no longer accessible to the public. Although it is at the top of the hill, it never runs dry so the water-table must be high in this area. The engraving shows other extensive formal gardens, each enclosed in a rectangle of hedges. The largest of these enclosures is intersected by strange serpentine paths.[3]

Bentinck loved straight lines; he came to an agreement with other local residents to straighten the narrow twisty lane which led to Windsor. He was interested in education and founded a school for both boys and girls in Bull Lane. There were to be twenty boys and

Hans William Bentinck, 1st Earl of Portland, K. G., 1649-1709 from a
painting by the studio of Hyacinthe Rigaud. The original painting is in the
National Portrait Gallery, London.

William, Prince of Orange, and H. W. Bentinck when both were recovering from smallpox, 1676, from a painting by H. Sneltens after Isaack Soubre. The original picture was (1914) the property of Baroness de Pallandt.

fifteen girls, all of whom were to be 'cloathed' and, after their time at school had ended, were to be apprenticed. He endowed the school and provided a salary of £20 each for the school master and school mistress. His care for the education of girls is remarkable at this time. Queen Anne admired Bentinck and came to visit him at Bulstrode. She created him Earl of Portland, and his son Henry, who succeeded him, became Duke.[4]

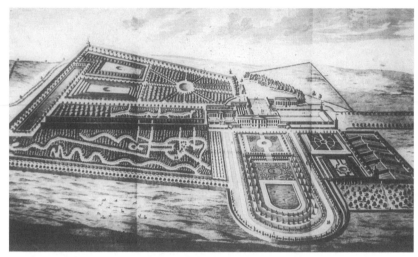

Engraving of the Formal Garden by Bowles about 1730.

Henry was very different from his father; he was renowned for the magnificence of the entertainments and his conviviality. He was deeply interested in painting. At this time it was fashionable for young men who went on the 'Grand Tour' to go to Venice and buy topological pictures. Henry, however, went further and persuaded Venetian artists to come to England. At the time a competition was arranged among artists from every country for plans for the decoration of St Paul's Cathedral. This was a great incentive for them to come to England. While here, they found plenty of work in decorating or

Chapel at Bulstrode House, designed by Sebastiano Ricci.

126

redecorating the many great houses built during this period.[5]

The Duke of Portland admired the work of Sebastiano Ricci and commissioned him to decorate the chapel at Bulstrode and also his town house. Sebastiano devised a unified plan for the decoration of the old chapel at Bulstrode. The walls were panelled with cedar elaborated with *trompe-l'œil* pilasters with allegorical figures supported on scrolled brackets. The scheme included two large paintings which represented the Baptism of Christ and the Last Supper. These were still in existence in 1847. A preliminary sketch for the Baptism was sold at Sotheby's in 1968 and is now in the possession of Mr John Harris, and that for the Last Supper is in the National Gallery of Art in Washington.[6]

Sebastiano also designed the stained glass windows in the chapel. When it was demolished, the Duke of Somerset had the windows taken to his West Country property of Maiden Bradley to be erected in the parish church. This building became unsafe, and one of the windows was taken to the church of St Andrew in the Wardrobe in the City.[7] Vertue, the eighteenth-century connoisseur who travelled throughout England and described works of art, says of the chapel, 'The whole is a noble free invention with a variety and freedom in the composition of the parts', while Horace Walpole reported in 1705 that there were two fine windows of modern glass in the chapel at Bulstrode.[8]

Stained glass window from the chapel of Bulstrode House now in the church of St. Andrew in the Wardrobe, City of London.

Lady Margaret (Peggy) Cavendish-Holles-Harley as a toddler, by Michael Dahl.

Duke Henry had a son called William who was a quiet pleasant young man. Dean Swift writes of him, 'he is free of the prevailing qualifications of the present young people of quality such as gaming, sharping [i.e. card sharping] and pilfering.' In the 1730s his family looked round for a suitable wife for him. At this time, marriages between the children of noble families required almost as much negotiation as those of ruling monarchs. It is not known how the Portlands came to choose Margaret, the only daughter of Edward Harley, as a suitable bride. She came of a distinguished family and was an heiress. The grandfather on her father's side was Robert

Harley, Lord Treasurer and faithful supporter of Queen Anne who was created Earl of Oxford. He possessed valuable property in London. His son Edward, Margaret's father, was less occupied in politics. He lived at Wimpole in Cambridgeshire and was in the process of rebuilding the house and remodelling the garden. He was a scholar and was considered rather pedantic as he was 'always talking of the Greeks and Romans out of season'. He had built up a magnificent library and was generous in allowing scholars and poets

Bust of Margaret Cavendish Harley aged eight by J.M. Rysbrack.

free access to it. These distinguished people usually stayed in the house. Among them were Pope, Prior, Richardson, Dr Middleton, a celebrated theologian, and Thomas Tredway, professor of music.[9]

Margaret's mother, Henrietta, was less remarkable than her father. Not very much is known about her except that she had red hair and that she and Edward Harley had been married quietly in the drawing room at Wimpole. She was very hospitable in entertaining all Edward's scholarly friends; she may have been rather prim as she disapproved of Pope who was 'too fond of philandering'.[10]

Margaret, also known as Peggy, was the only child of Edward and Henrietta. She was much loved in the great Cambridgeshire house and no doubt sometimes entered the library where scholars and poets would be at work. Swift might have formed one of the group, but Matthew Prior, a rather pedestrian poet, seems to have been her favourite. He addressed a poem to her:

> To lift your heart and hands to Heaven
> and, dearest child, along the way
> in everything you do or say
> obey and please my lord and lady
> so God shall love and angels aid thee.

Peggy's grandfather, Robert Harley the distinguished statesman, used to write to Peggy's mother to enquire about her health. On one occasion the reply came, 'she has cut two teeth as easy as can be', and on another her mother reported, 'she is backward of her feet and also her tongue but, at three, Miss Peggy is of perfect health and wantonness and promises, as far as any lady of her years, to be an admirable coquette.'[11]

There is a delightful portrait of her as a toddler and another,[12] when she was older, in which she is dressed as a shepherdess. The outstanding work of art which she inspired was a bust carved by Rysbrack when she was twelve years old. (The late Duke of Portland, a distinguished soldier and administrator, told me that, on his way to breakfast, he always kissed her.) Rysbrack was a Dutch sculptor who came to England and was responsible for some of the best large-scale monuments in English churches.[13]

Not much is known about Peggy's formal education; she probably had a governess and visiting masters to teach her dancing, French and Italian. She joined in the social life of Cambridgeshire. Her special friend was Elizabeth Collingwood who also lived in Cambridgeshire. She was four years younger than Margaret. Elizabeth was an excellent and witty letter-writer. Margaret used to lament that her talents did not lie in this direction and that her letters were 'hum-drum'. She was more interested in the natural

Judge Sir George Jeffreys, 1st Baron Jeffreys, as Recorder of London, attrib. to William Claret. Natural Portrait Gallery.

world than in literature. However, she had a great sense of humour; in the letters she exchanged with Miss Collingwood ('Colly' or 'Cauliflower', they always disguised the names of their families and acquaintances with nicknames).[14] Her friends referred to her as the Merry Duchess or the Sprightly Duchess. Mrs Delany recounts how, when the two of them were making nets for the cherry trees, 'a laugh would be hatched' and the work laid aside.[15]

Margaret was twenty years old when the negotiations for her marriage took place; she seems to have accepted the arrangement without protest. The young couple were married in Marylebone chapel in Vere Street, a simple building with a classical façade. The street had recently been built to serve the great estate between Marylebone Road and Oxford Street; this area was owned by the Portlands and was just being developed (the street names bear testimony to the connection of the family with this area: e.g. Harley Street, Henrietta Street, Welbeck Street, Portland Square, and also Bulstrode Court.) On the occasion of the marriage, Margaret had an elaborate trousseau which included:[16]

one gown and petticoat of white Paduasoy [a smooth silk originally made in Padua] embroidered with gold and all colours
one gown and petticoat of pink armeseen both gown and petticoat covered all over with rich silver trimming mixed with coloured flowers

William, 2nd Duke of Portland, K.G., 1709-62. Lady Margaret Cavendish-Holles-Harley, Duchess of Portland, 1715-85, from enamels by C. F. Zincke.

gown and petticoat of white lutestring [a glossy silk cloth] clouded with pink and brown night gown of yellow lutestring ruches fine calico quilted bed gown
double mob [cap?] and double ruffling and ruche laced all round with 'maclean' lace, the pattern being of oak leaves
14 tuckers of plain cambric
30 pocket handkerchiefs
2 laced riding skirts
2 pair of scarlet stockings
28 day shifts
3 white calico quilted petticoats to wear over hoops
1 hoop of white lutestring
silver tissue shoes
blue velvet clogs
2 pair of stays
6 fine holland aprons.

The occurrence of the holland aprons among the finery shows that she intended following active pursuits. Her trousseau is moderate in comparison with that of the Duchess of Devonshire: besides all kinds of gowns, cloaks, etc., she had sixty five pairs of shoes and forty five pairs of stockings.[17]

William and Margaret set up house in Bulstrode in 1732 and seemed very happy. Writing to one of her friends, Margaret called her husband 'sweet William' and said 'this is a flower with which I wish you were better acquainted'. William did his best to entertain the ladies; one day he took them round London to show them the sights.

William's father died shortly after William and Margaret came to Bulstrode, so they inherited the title and became Duke and Duchess of Portland. They also inherited a large house within the precincts of Whitehall. Margaret's friend Elizabeth Robinson came to stay at Bulstrode and wrote to another friend, exclaiming in ecstasy, 'The rural beauties of this place would pursuade [sic] me that I was in the plains of Arcadia but the magnificence of the building under whose gilded roof I dwell has a pomp far from pastoral. We go to chapel twice a week and have sermons on Sundays for His Grace values the title of Christian above that of Duke. We breakfast at nine, dine at two, drink tea at eight and sup at ten. We work or read in the morning, the same in the afternoon, walk from six until supper and then write letters which the Duke comes in to frank.'[18] [Members of both houses of Parliament were able to stamp letters which then went free.]

The Duke and Duchess took religion very seriously. They went to church regularly, and there were frequent services in the Bulstrode chapel when the whole party assembled in the gallery and went down into the body of the chapel to receive communion. Their

Portrait commissioned by King George III from J. Opie of 'dearest Mrs Delany'. It is on indefinite loan to Bevingborough Hall, near York.

tastes in literature and music were strict and conservative. They liked *Clarissa* by Richardson but deplored Sterne's *Tristram Shandy*. They attended oratorios when they were in London and especially admired Handel's *Messiah*. The Duchess was upset because the populace preferred *The Beggar's Opera*.

Soon after William and Margaret came to Bulstrode, Margaret contracted a close friendship with a lady called Mrs Pendarves who, on her second marriage, became Mrs Delany.[19] She was older than Margaret and had been a friend of her mother. She was a lady of wit and learning and was held in high regard by society. It is through her eyes that Bulstrode can be seen, for the friendship between the Duchess and Mrs Delany is celebrated in verse.

The same desire, the same ingenious arts
Delighted both, we owned and blessed the power
That joined at once our studies and our hearts.[20]

As will be seen below, botany was the favourite pursuit, but they were skilful in all arts and hobbies. They both spoke French and Italian fluently and they were adept at spinning, embroidery and drawing; they produced very fine shell-work and wood-turning and they also tried to learn mathematics and astronomy.

In 1737 the Duke and Duchess began a family. The first child was called Elizabeth. Presumably like the Duchess's other children, she was fed by a wet nurse but when she was a toddler she played in the great house and helped to amuse the guests. Mrs Delany, who was staying at Bulstrode, wrote enthusiastically, 'We have a variety of amusements as reading, working and drawing in the morning; in the afternoon the scene changes, there are billiards, looking over prints, coffee, tea and, by way of interlude, pretty Lady Betty comes on the stage and I can play as well at Bo Peep as if I had a nursery of my own. She is the best humoured little thing I ever knew.' (Later, Elizabeth married Lord Weymouth who became Marquis of Bath).[21]

There were three other children: Harriet who became Countess of Stamford, William Henry, the future third Duke who was called Lord Titchfield during his minority, Margaret who died young, and Edward. When the Duchess was pregnant she sent for Elizabeth Collingwood to attend her, for it was customary when a lady of quality was pregnant for her to have a younger lady with her who accompanied her everywhere and had to be suitably dressed. Elizabeth wrote to her father saying that never again would she so need a handsome suit as on this occasion when appearing with the Duchess; her father sent £20 and the Duchess helped her to lay out the money to the best advantage. They chose a silk, a 'little imperfect in the weaving' and also a 'hoop of the greatest magnitude'.[22]

Most of the Duchess's children were born without difficulty, but when she was pregnant with Margaret she decided to go to London, probably to be treated by Dr Mead, the most famous women's doctor of the time. He followed the barbarous practice of bleeding; Margaret's friends almost despaired of her recovery, and the Duke sent a pathetic ill-spelt letter to Mrs Delany to prepare her for the worst. Eventually Margaret and the new baby recovered.[23]

Meanwhile, with this increasing family William and Margaret decided to look for a governess and chose a lady called Mrs Elstob (though unmarried) who, with her brother, had published the first Anglo-Saxon dictionary and various important Anglo-Saxon texts. After her brother died, poor Mrs Elstob tried to keep a school for tradesmen's daughters. She found the work so hard that she had no time to 'eat or drink, much less to study'. Friends tried to obtain a post for her in a noble family; she wrote deprecatingly that she could not do any work proper to her sex, although she added that her dress was of her own weaving and that she wore no stockings but what she had knitted herself. Although she must have been rather depressing to look at, the Duchess, who appreciated her genuine scholarship, was glad to employ her. She was a great success; she loved the Duchess and says, 'The children by their sweet endearing temper clearly discover whose children they are.' The children loved her and called her 'Tob'. She lived happily in the great house, although becoming increasingly crippled by arthritis. She was able to continue her Anglo-Saxon studies. A scholar called Rowe More reported that he visited her 'sleeping room and found her surrounded by books and dirtiness, the usual appendages of people of learning'. In her later years either Elizabeth or Harriet penned letters at her dictation because of her arthritis.[24]

Things went on quietly until one terrible Christmas when, as Mrs Delany says, 'The young people full of joy and spirits had a little dancing', Lord Edward being 'very brisk'. Next day he had a headache and felt tired. A doctor was sent for from Windsor, who diagnosed smallpox. The Duchess tried to keep up her spirits. Lord Edward recovered but the girls caught it, and Mrs Delany had her harpsichord moved into the sick room to try to soothe Harriet whose illness was the most serious.[25] It is surprising that the Duchess and her children were not vaccinated. Vaccination was known at the time and many people underwent it, but the Duchess was conservative. She recommended all kinds of herbal cures and believed in old wives' tales. For instance, a prescription for a cough was two or three snails boiled in water, and for croup a spider sealed in a goose quill hung round the neck.[26]

In spite of her fondness for Bulstrode and her preoccupation with her family, Margaret played a very important part in the social life of

London and of the Court. She was friendly with George III and Queen Charlotte.

Women's costume at this time was elaborate. The hair was dressed high (cartoons show men on ladders powdering the top) and was filled with ornaments such as ships or birds. Ladies wore gowns which were draped over hoops at the back and open down

Reconstruction of the court dress designed and embroided by Mrs Delany for herself, with photograph of the stomacher decorated by pinks and lily-of-the-valley.

137

Detail of embroidery on Mrs. Delany's court dress.

Caricatures of contemporary fastions: a hairdresser on ladder powdering top of a lady's wig and people tight-lacing a lady.

the front to show embroidered petticoats. The gowns were also open above the waist and very often a richly decorated 'stomacher' was worn.[27]

Mrs Delany said that the Duchess had twelve 'toilettes'. When she went to the Queen's birthday and took her daughter Elizabeth to court for the first time, she wore a dress of white and silver flowered with gold and silver and a white satin stomacher covered with jewels of all colours, and all her diamonds. Lady Betty wore a stomacher of blue satin with loops and stars of diamonds and a dress of white and silver flowered with silver and blue. Before being presented she practised dancing with a train. 'She was an engaging figure', wrote Mrs Delany, 'she looked so modest and composed although glittering with diamonds.'

No doubt the Duchess and Lady Betty looked charming, but some of the clothes must have been very ugly, such as the gown worn by Lady Huntingdon at the Prince of Wales's birthday. This had a black velvet petticoat which was decorated with a large stone vase filled with ramping flowers.[28]

The family travelled between the London house at Whitehall and Bulstrode very frequently. The roads were bad and there were many accidents. The bridge over the river Colne at Uxbridge was under construction in the 1760s and the water often overflowed. Anne Granville, Mrs Delany's niece, described a journey to Bulstrode when 'we flounced into great holes of ice and snow – enough to swallow up coach and horses'.[29] The coaches often overturned. The family used to set out from London about 10 o'clock and arrive at Bulstrode for a very substantial meal at about three o'clock.

Formal meals consisted of numerous courses. Each course was virtually a complete meal: meat, poultry and sweets. Thus, a meal whose menu has been preserved had 'in the first course fish, beef-steaks, soup, rabbits and onions, fillet of veal, blancmange, cherries, Dutch cheeses and the second course turkey pout, salmon, quailles, little terrenes, peas, mushrooms, apple pye; then there was desserts raspberries and cream, sweetmeats and jelly, strawberries and cream, almond cream, currants and gooseberries, orange butter.'[30] Generally, however, the meals were simpler. Mrs Delany was fond of oysters and she and the Duchess often dined off sprats.

The Duchess's chief helper was John Lightfoot, curate at Uxbridge and a distinguished botanist. The Duke had appointed him chaplain at Bulstrode where he took services twice a week in the chapel. Any time which he could spare from his duties in Uxbridge were spent at Bulstrode where he instructed the Duchess in botany and helped her to collect plants. He was elected a member of the Royal Society and he corresponded with Linnaeus, the outstanding botanist of the time who had introduced the first systematic classification of plants. Another helper was Dr Solander who had studied with Linnaeus. When he came to England, the Duchess brought him to Bulstrode and taught him English. He became assistant librarian at the British Museum which at this time was devoted only to natural history. A more practical helper was

George Dionysius Ehret who had been a nurseryman at Heidelberg. He had a wonderful talent for representing plants and painted for her some 300 exotic and 500 English plants, done on vellum and highly finished. He also taught her daughters.[31]

Mrs Delany was also very interested in botany, but perhaps from an aesthetic rather than a scientific angle. She used to attend the discussion and gently mocked the serious scholars, both for their extraordinary names and their scientific vocabulary. As she says, 'an ignorant person sitting by might expect to see their candles to turn blue and that they were at their incantations.' On another occasion she simply says, 'Mr Lightfoot and Botany go on as usual.'

The Duchess often used to visit Weymouth, the seat of her son-in-law. We hear of her scrambling among the rocks to collect shells, seaweed, fossils. She brought back sea creatures of the 'polibus kind' and a green worm larger than a centipede. The creatures were kept alive in sea water brought to Bulstrode.[32]

There was by now a very large collection of botanical and geological specimens – especially shells – at Bulstrode, for friends sent her interesting objects, both from this country and overseas. She also bought specimens from dealers who flourished at this time; she loved objects from exotic countries. She was acknowledged as an authority on shells, and the University of Oxford dedicated a comprehensive book on conchology to her.[33]

Another place she loved to visit was Calwich in Shropshire where Mrs Delany's brother, also a botanist, had an estate. Here she met the French philosopher Rousseau and they used to study plants together. He used to send specimens back to Bulstrode and they carried on a friendly correspondence.[34]

Even Bulstrode was not large enough to house the collection. In 1769 they were gathering mushrooms and fungi which grew prolifically in Bulstrode and the commons round about. Mrs Delany describes the breakfast room which is now 'turned into a depository of sieves, pans, platters and productions of that nature spread on tables, windows, chairs with books opened at their usual places [which] make an agreeable confusion and sometimes, not with-standing twelve chairs and a couch, it is a little difficult to find a seat.'[35]

The Duke died in 1761 and Dr Delany in 1768 so both ladies were now widows. Their friendship grew even stronger, and Mrs Delany usually spent the six summer months of the year at Bulstrode. They used to walk about the park or drive in a chaise. Mrs Delany wrote descriptions to her friends thus in 1779:

> such woods and groves and lawns and terraces not to be described and all enlivened with such a variety of animals hardly

to be enumerated – beautiful deer, oxen cows sheep of all countries, bufaloes, mouflons, horses, asses; all in their proper places. Then hares and squirrels at every step you take so confident of their security that they hardly run away. The great lawn before the house is the nursery of all sorts of pheasants and pea fowl and guinea fowl besides interlopers of bantam pigeons; and not withstanding these numerous families the lawn is kept with as much neatness as the drawing room.

Or again:

The D. and I took a short walk and a pretty uncommon scene is before me: on the lawn of a flock of sheep, a shepherd and a dog; at a little distance and in the foreground fifteen or sixteen hares feeding with peacocks and guinea fowl that makes a beautiful mixture of pretty objects . . .

Recording another walk round the grounds she says, 'nothing pleased me more than the gold and silver fish I have seen in shoals, thousands I am sure, all swimming up to the D. who fed them with bread.'

Most of the animals were in cages, including a porcupine and a Java hare, but others ranged freely. The menagerie was a notable feature of Bulstrode. It had been begun by the first Duke who had macaws, parrots and all sorts of foreign birds flying in one of the woods. He built a house and kept people to wait on them. Many of

A drawing by Mrs Delany of Bulstrode's park.

Bulstrode House from East – probably early eighteenth century.

the exhibits had died, but the Duchess restocked the wood and park, as Mrs Montagne said, 'The Dss is as eager on collecting animals as if she foresaw another deluge and was assembling every creature after its kind to preserve the species.'[36]

The high point in their study of natural history was reached when Captain Cook, Joseph Banks and Dr Solander returned from the first of their sensational voyages round the world, bringing many interesting and exotic plants with them, especially from the South Seas.[37] They came to Bulstrode in November 1771, and Mrs Delany reports that there were many learned discussions in which Mr Lightfoot joined. They talked of how the account of the voyage should be published. The Duchess was given seeds from some of the plants, and it is possible that some of these were grown at Bulstrode, for an old map marks a field called 'Botany Bay field'.

Soon after this party at Bulstrode, the Duchess and Mrs Delany went to the British Museum where Dr Solander took them round and showed them interesting specimens. They also went to Mr Banks's house in New Burlington Street where many other specimens were preserved. Mrs Delany describes their visit a 'a charming entertainment of activities'.[38]

The Duchess was an active gardener, and during the cold weather she 'heaped cloaks on cloaks'. She was expert in propagating especially by layering. She had a flourishing vegetable garden, but her chief interest was a scientifically designed garden, probably inspired by Miller, the head of the Chelsea Physic Garden 'where every species of plant was planted separately according to its species'.[39]

Her favourite gardener was called Mr Agnew. He helped her with the work and also found specimens for her. Local people also brought her plants and birds, birds' eggs and nests, including eggs of the crown bird and a reed warbler's nest, but when someone brought her young nightingales, she let them go.

Mrs Delany meanwhile began a new project, although she was now seventy-two years of age. As already shown, the Duchess had built up a comprehensive herbarium with the aid of Ehret. Now Mrs Delany did the same thing but used her new technique of cutting out paper flowers and mounting them on black backgrounds. In order to so this she studied the flowers most minutely, not only their petals but also their stamens, calyxes, leaves, veins and prickles on their stalks. She used to go to the ports and buy thin tissue paper from the sailors who brought it from China. Sometimes, however, she dyed the paper herself. The background was usually coloured with Indian ink. She used to cut out the tiny fragments of coloured paper very precisely without drawing them first. In her picture of the 'melon thistle' the flower is made up of 190 parts and there are 399 spines on the stem. Often, as in the feathered pink, the petals are almost thread-like and swirl about. One cannot help admiring the exquisite fineness and sharpness of the scissors which she used. The 'paper mosaicks', as Mrs Delany called them, were much admired by the experts,

'Paper mosaicks' by Mrs Delany: left, *Lilium Canadense* (Lilium superbum); right, *rosa pendulina*.

143

especially the great painter Reynolds, and Sir Joseph Banks, who said that they were the only 'imitations of Nature he had ever seen from which he could venture to describe botanically any plant without the least fear of committing an error'.[40]

Although the Duchess's main interest was in the natural world, she also collected pictures, enamels and china. She had inherited a fine collection of works of art and pictures from her father, Edward Harley. Her collection included a Holy Family by Raphael, a sleeping boy by Van Dyck, paintings by Claude Lorain and Elscheimer, and also Rembrandt engravings. One of the chief treasures was the *Bedford Book of Hours* illuminated in the fifteenth century. The chief addition made by the Duchess was the blue intaglio Roman vase which had been acquired by Sir William Hamilton. The arrangements for the sale were very intricate and were helped by Sir William's famous wife, Emma,[41] and also by Mary Hamilton, his niece who stayed at Bulstrode and was a great favourite with both the Duchess and Mrs Delany.

A good deal of information about the collection can be gleaned from the letters of Horace Walpole and the journals of Vertue.[42] When the Duke and Duchess first went to Bulstrode Walpole described the 'brave gallery of old pictures'. It is probable that this gallery ran behind the main gallery and its auxiliary rooms which faced south across the park. In 1762 he reported that the Duchess had 'lately enriched him exceedingly' by the gift of nine portraits of the court of Louis Quatorze, and went on to say that Lord Portland brought them over, that they hung in the nursery and that 'the children amused themselves with shooting at them'. Walpole had a rather ambiguous relationship with the Duchess, not unmixed with envy. He said of her, 'she is perfectly sober and only loves empty vases'. When a copy of the King of France's Raphael came up for sale at Christie's and was bought by the Duchess for the phenomenal sum of £7,000, Walpole said that the bidding was carried on by the Duchess and other members of the nobility who 'care not what they pay'.[43] Although he was often sarcastic and rather disagreeable, he was regarded with great respect during his lifetime. He disliked the classical architecture so characteristic of the eighteenth century and advocated a return to Gothic as more romantic.

The great example for this transformation was set by his own house at Strawberry Hill, where he himself often posed as a monk in his little Gothic chapel. We hear how in June 1770 the Duchess and Mrs Delany went to Strawberry Hill and how, a few days later, he came to Bulstrode 'where all was hurry and excitement', and plans were set afoot for transforming the house into a Gothic mansion. The Duchess began in a small way by having a grotto built at the head of the Long Water. Mrs Delany supervised the work; she says that 'the stones were ruder than Gothic and the stone-mason's head harder than the stones he hammers'. When finished it was a remarkable structure; its rough stones were overlaid by delicate shell-work in which Mrs Delany excelled.[44] The Duchess used to love sitting at the entrance, spinning at her wheel or practising her skills in wood-turning.

There was a growing intimacy between the ladies at Bulstrode and George III and Queen Charlotte at Windsor. This was made easy because the Duchess's daughter, Lady Weymouth, was a lady-

Horace Walpole, 4th Earl of Orford, by John Giles Eccardt, 1754. National Portrait Gallery.

Grotto built by under the supervision of the Duchess of Portland and Mrs. Delany.

Silhouette by Mrs Delany, of a game of chess and a lady tambouring. The silhouette on the left is probably Thomas Thynne 3rd Viscount Weymouth, later 1st Marquess of Both.

in-waiting. Visits were often exchanged. One of the most notable was on the birthday of the Prince of Wales in August 1778. The celebrations began early when a cavalcade of fifty persons drove through the park and round the courtyard up to the house. The Duchess waited on the hall steps at the main entrance. The Royals 'walked through the great apartments and admired everything they

Frontispiece from Skinner & Co.'s auction catalogue of the Duchess of Portland's collection, 1786, in which the Portland Vase takes pride of place.

saw, the young ones full of observation and proper questions, some whistling, some skipping ... charmed with the excellent breakfast and eat abundantly'. This breakfast was spread in the gallery which ran the length of the south façade and out of which opened a suite of eight rooms and three closets. 'The tables were spread with tea, coffee, chocolate and cakes fruit and ices to which succeeded, as if by magic a cold repast. The Queen sat meanwhile in the drawing room at the end of the great gallery. She was dressed in an Italian nightgown of purple lute-string trimmed with silver gauze and a hat. The Duchess brought her tea and biscuits. The Queen insisted on taking back the cup to the gallery herself.' She especially admired the chairs worked from nature in chenille by Mrs Delany.[45]

The return visit was equally successful; there was music and also dancing for the younger people and much conversation. George III loved music and had a special interest in that of Handel. There was dancing for the young, but after a time the King stopped it because he thought that the musicians would be getting tired. The whole party then walked outside on the south terrace because the King said that the people of Windsor liked to see them. The Duchess's party returned to Bulstrode by torchlight.[46]

Somewhat later, when the Duchess was an old lady of sixty-eight and Mrs Delany eighty-two, a stag hunt was organized on the common. The Duchess was no early riser but she got into her chaise at quarter to ten and went to Gerrards Cross 'about the middle of the common'. The King came a quarter of an hour later with the Prince of Wales and a large retinue. They saw the stag turned out of a cart and the 'poor trembling creature bounding over the plain in the hope of escaping his pursuers'. The Duchess hurried back to Bulstrode to receive the Queen, who stayed until two o'clock. The Lady Mary Forbes entertained a large party at the Bull.[47]

Life went on happily. We will leave the old ladies sitting at small tables with their work and separate candles. There was much conversation from grave to gay. One of the subjects which interested them was the invention of air balloons. Mrs Delany was older than the Duchess but in better health.[48] The Duchess died in 1785 and, in spite of the great wealth which she inherited, she was bankrupt and her whole collection had to be sold.

The sale, which was conducted by Skinner & Co., contained over 4,000 items and lasted for thirty-eight days. Mr Lightfoot drew up the catalogue which is, in itself, a landmark in the history of botany, as many plants received their names and classification for the first time. He says, 'It was the intention of the enlightened possessor to have had unknowen [sic] species described and published ... but it pleased God to shorten her design.' There is a copy of the catalogue in the British Library. The engraving on the cover shows a most extraordinary jumble of objects; the centrepiece is the Portland vase with a branch of coral projecting from its mouth. The vase fetched £1,029.[49]

5

Bulstrode in the Nineteenth and Twentieth Centuries

After the death of the Duchess in 1785 and the sale of her great collection, William Henry Bentinck, Marquess of Tichborne, her eldest son, inherited Bulstrode. He and the Duchess had never been on good terms, partly through political differences. She was a 'dyed in the wool' Tory and a great friend of Lady Bute whose husband, Lord Bute, had been George III's tutor and whom he personally appointed as Prime Minister in 1762. Bute was a leading Tory and an upholder of royal power but William, now Duke of Portland, was an important member of the Whig party and closely connected with the Cavendish family who wielded enormous power at this time.[1] He had never liked Bulstrode and had exchanged the estate for that of Welbeck in Nottinghamshire which the Duchess had inherited

The 3rd Duke of Portland, in front of the riding school and stables at Welbeck Abbey, from a painting by George Stubbs 1767.

149

from her mother, Henrietta, who was herself a Cavendish.[2] William lived with Henrietta, his grandmother, and married Lady Dorothy Cavendish, the fourth daughter of the Duke of Devonshire; he was thus absorbed into the more liberal faction of the Whig party headed by the Marquess of Rockingham.

William was a quiet man who lacked energy, but was welcomed enthusiastically as one of the most important members of the party, partly because of his connection with the Cavendishes. He was known as a 'convenient cipher'. He took office under Rockingham in 1765 and again in 1782. His liberal views are illustrated by his support of Wilkes who had attacked the king in an article in his newspaper called *The North Briton*. Wilkes and many of his supporters were imprisoned but Wilkes claimed immunity because he was an MP. This case was of great significance to the Whigs, and William illuminated his London house in celebration of Wilkes's discharge.

After the death of Rockingham, William became Prime Minister, presiding over an uncomfortable coalition of Fox and North. After a few months he honourably resigned because the King and the Lords refused to accept a bill regulating the government of India which had been passed by the Commons.[3]

Although politics was probably his prime interest, he also spent time and energy in the rebuilding of the Jeffreys' house at Bulstrode and 'improving' the park. The first architect whom he consulted was John Nash, who designed the Nash Terraces in Regent's Park. Three plans were exhibited in the Royal Academy in 1802. They show the Jeffreys' house deprived of its pediment and fronted by an unbroken colonnade. It was roofed by a dome and had orangeries on each end. This Nash plan was not carried out, but there is an imaginary painting of it at Welbeck Abbey. The Duke preferred a rival scheme by James Wyatt which was more romantic. The easiest way to read these plans is to imagine oneself standing in the chapel which occupied the south-west corner of the building and was entered from the end of Jeffreys' long gallery; as shown above, it survived from the early seventeenth century and probably remained unaltered until the final rebuilding in the mid-nineteenth century. The great gallery was divided up and the pediment demolished. The central part of the gallery was converted into a large library, and a state dining room was constructed at the east end and a smaller room to the west. A large square tower occupied the south-west corner in front of the chapel and two smaller rectangular towers flanked a new entrance on the south front. These towers formed hexagonal bay windows to the library on the first floor. In the engraving the east end of the south front seems to survive from the older building as the windows are similar and it consisted of only two storeys whereas the rest of this wing has had another storey added to it which, like the towers, was topped by battlements. The

Plan by John Nash for the rebuilding of Bulstrode House, exhibited in 1802.

greatest modification, however, was on the west front where a large new wing with towers was built in front of the Jeffreys' building. The centre part of the first floor was occupied by a sitting room which had bedrooms and dressing rooms on either side. The ground floor was used as cellars and storerooms. The size of this new wing can be appreciated, for the entrance is clearly the now detached building known as the 'Pigeon Tower' which became

Plan for rebuilding Bulstrode House by James Wyatt, 1802.

151

View by John Buckler, 1818, of James Wyatt's rebuilding of the south wing.

isolated in 1860. Legend has grown up round the building, and it is sometimes called the Norman Tower, connecting it with the ancient legend. It is built of pleasant softly coloured red brick and clearly dates from about 1800 – presumably this material was also used for the rest of the house.[4]

Before the building work was begun, the Duke began to remodel the park. He called in Humphry Repton, one of the most prominent landscape designers of the period. Writing in 1802, Repton describes this work as 'opening up the valleys and taking away a great depth of earth from the stems of the largest trees, which had

View of Wyatt's rebuidling from the south east, showing the remains of Jeffreys' house

The arms from the monument of the 12th Duke of Somerset, in the churchyard of St. James's Church, Gerrards Cross.

Bulstrode House, rebuilt by Benjamin Ferry 1855-62, the north-east front.

153

Ferry's rebuilt house, from the south-west.

Garden entrance of extension by James Wyatt, known as The Pigeon Tower.

been formerly buried', and thus 'by degrees restoring the surface of the ground to its original and natural shape'. In a note, Repton adds, 'in this great work are occasionally employed among the more efficient labourers, an hundred children from ten to fifteen years old, who are thus early trained in habits of wholesome industry far different from the foul air and confinement of spinning in a cotton mill; to the benevolent observer no object can be more delightful than park scenery thus animated'. (These were perhaps pauper children.) Repton also designed a great drive, going round the park and running along the top of the ramparts of the camp which he called 'a circumstance of antiquity worthy to be drawn into note.'[5]

The rebuilding and remodelling of the house and park were only partially carried out because the Duke became bankrupt and died in 1809 owing Wyatt large sums. The fourth duke was not interested in the estate so he sold it with its unfinished buildings to the eleventh Duke of Somerset. The new owner commissioned plans for the rebuilding by Francis Sandys and Robert Smirke, and in 1819 a plan by P.F. Robinson was exhibited in the Royal Academy. The Duke preferred still another plan by Wyattville, nephew of James Wyatt and rebuilder of Windsor Castle, but none of these plans was carried out.[6]

Edward Augustus Seymour, the eleventh Duke, like the Portlands was a man of intellectual pursuits. He was interested in botany and was a member of the Royal Society, the Linnean Society, the Zoological Society and was President of the Royal Institution. He was also a liberal politician and held various offices. He wrote mathematical, theological and political treatises. His two sons died unmarried during his lifetime, and the dukedom devolved on his two brothers successively.[7]

In spite of his many interests he loved Bulstrode. Writing to his brother in 1813 he says, 'I hope that you have run down to Bulstrode to enjoy its delightful shades. I could wish myself in the lime walk with you.'[8] (This is the lime avenue which still survives.) But he seems to have despaired of making the house habitable. In 1814 he thought of selling it, and a catalogue was prepared. This describes a noble walled garden, the pleasure grounds tastefully disposed with rarest exotic trees, the gardens with an ornamental sheet of water, a Turkish pavilion, a Dutch cottage, a conservatory and a gardener's house, 'the whole', as the catalogue says, 'disposed with the hand of taste in a very superior style of elegance'. The house was hardly habitable; the purchaser could either take the mansion or any part of it or sell the materials by auction.[9]

A plan which was prepared for taxation purposes a few years later recommends that the great tower on the south-east corner, the central part of the 'old house' and the new building, not yet floored, should be taken down. It says that the east and west wings which

Staircase and hall of Bulstrode House, 1897.

156

were new and fit for habitation were let as a farm. The Duke died in 1855 and his successor, the twelfth Duke, proceeded with the complete rebuilding of the house. Disregarding the plans already made, he employed the architect Benjamin Ferry who was a pupil of Pugin and is chiefly known as a builder of churches, some of which, like that at Penn Street, are simple and attractive.[10] Ferry was known locally, as he very sensitively enlarged and remodelled Upton church. The house was finished in 1862 and has remained virtually unaltered. It is built of peculiarly hard, bright red brick (quite unlike that used by either Jeffreys or Wyatt). There is an imposing courtyard on the north side. This is dominated by a tall tower, which fulfils the useful function of accommodating large tanks into which water used to be pumped from a deep well. At the top of the tower there is a sculptured bull. The arched entrance to the house is placed in the centre of this north front. On the east of this courtyard are stables which are elaborately treated.

The rest of the house is even more ornate, and is designed with an abundance of gables and towers. Not very much is known about the original decoration and fittings, for the interior was modernized in 1910 by Eden but a few excellent photographs exist. The description of the interior given here depends partly on a catalogue prepared in 1932 for a sale of the house which was not carried through, and partly by my recollections.

The front entrance on the north opens into a lobby, and this leads to a large square hall with a wide staircase and gallery; the wood-work is an unpleasant, highly polished pitch-pine and is partly supported by Corinthian columns. Doors into the various rooms open into this hall. To the north are a large dining-room with a beamed ceiling and a smoking-room; the more attractive rooms face south and have the same delightful view as the great gallery of the Jeffreys' house. There are three rooms on this side; the first is a fine L-shaped library, the second a drawing-room and the third the boudoir. They all open on to a colonnaded terrace which is raised above the level of the garden by a wisteria-covered wall. The columns are coupled and have elaborately carved capitals rather like those in the stable-block. These rooms and some of the bedrooms above have marble mantelpieces which might have come from the Wyatt house; also, opening on the hall is a staircase leading downwards to another wing in which there was the billiard room and several other rooms. The kitchen was very large and had a glass roof and big kitchen ranges. Altogether there were ten reception rooms, sixteen bedrooms, seventeen servants' bedrooms and nine bathrooms.

The Duke, whose elaborate marble monument stands in the churchyard of St James' church in Gerrards Cross, died in 1883. He liked Bulstrode and spent much time there. He encouraged local

Above: The terrace on the south front. Below: Bulstrode House, staircase hall from the staircase, 1897.

Photograph of the corridor leading from the main entrance to the east wing, 1897.

Photograph of the corridor to the north main entrance, 1897. The corridor to the front entrance is to the left.

people to come into the park and he founded the cricket club; he was, however, a strict landlord. There were many tenants of the estate in Chalfont St Peter, Chalfont St Giles, Fulmer, etc., and we hear how the tenants 'attended on Tuesday and paid rent. In January 1866 Mr Hock came to the rent dinner making the one hundreth half year he has paid his rent. We have letters from a young man begging to be allowed to succeed his father at the post office.' There is a beautifully written letter from William Bell, the blacksmith, complaining of having had notice to quit for no reason. The bailiff recounts how some boys who had been caught setting the common on fire were imprisoned for one month with hard labour, while a man was condemned to ten years' hard labour for poaching and shooting at the under keeper after visiting a beer shop at Hedgerley. These documents also tell how angry the freeholders at Fulmer had become because it was proposed to set up two new beer shops in the village, the three existing ones being quite adequate to serve the 350 inhabitants. We hear how some of the labourers on the estate were annoyed at not being given a holiday for a wedding.[11]

The main events of the Duke's time at Bulstrode were the enclosure of 'Fulmer Common', the wooded area south of the A40, now known as Dukes Wood. Although this was common land, several people had built cottages there. The Duke applied for an enclosure bill which was passed by Parliament. This showed a valuation of the land and of the rights of the cottagers. As in mediaeval times, testimony was taken from 'old witnesses' and the parish books. Eventually all was settled and the bailiff wrote to the Duke saying, 'I think that the Bulstrode allotment is all your Grace could wish but it is difficult to please all.' The land was never brought under cultivation but provided good shooting, especially when a large number of rhododendron bushes were planted to provide cover for the pheasants. This explains the splendid display of rhododendrons still flowering in the gardens facing the A40 and the Windsor Road.

Connected with this enclosure was the building of St James' church. Colonel Reid and his two unmarried sisters for some time rented a derelict part of Bulstrode House, but then moved to the Pickerage farm in Fulmer. The colonel died and his sisters wanted to build a church for Gerrards Cross in his memory. They asked the Duke to give them a site on the newly enclosed Fulmer common. This request at first was startling, for it was not clear whether the Duke would be within his rights to make such a grant. The Duke's agent strongly recommended him to agree, saying, 'It would be decidedly to the advantage of your property, as adding respectability in that locality ... and it would be an everlasting and distinct confirmation of your title to the manor.' So much for the eulogy in the document called the *First Sabbath* written to mark the dedication of the church by the Bishop of Oxford which mentions 'the Holy plot of land which has never been bought or sold'. The Misses Reid had promised to bear the whole expense of building the church. They employed a well known architect, unfortunately called Tite, who had rebuilt the Bank of England in the City of London in the classical style. It is said that the ladies asked him to tour Italy to find the most beautiful building and to use it as a model. It is believed that he chose Florence cathedral with Giotto's tower, but he came back and used yellow brick with red brick patterns instead of the black and white marble of the original. This may well not be true as there are other Italian churches to which St James is more similar.[12]

It is interesting to look at the household accounts between about 1860 and the First World War. They were carefully kept by the bailiff, and by the formidable housekeeper Mrs Solley who took them up to London to the estate office every month. She travelled by omnibus, probably from Uxbridge. In 1860 Mr Grimsdale was the head gardener and had a staff of eleven under him. He received £1 5s as his wage. The number of gardeners increased later to twenty. The nine grooms each received 14s a week; two sawyers, two bricklayers and two carpenters received wages which varied from 11s to £1 10s per week. Young boys received 1d to 3/6 per hour. The money to pay the outside workers varied from £27 to £36 per week.

Indoors there was a staff of 25. Their wages are not specified but in 1863 Mrs Solley received £320 for wages and board wages. From the tradesmen's bills the food consumed seems lavish: £250 for the butcher, although some of the supplies must have been home-produced, £44 for the baker and £47 for 100 lbs of Twinings tea. The farming seems to have been on a small scale; £51 was received for cattle, £15 for wool, £5 for skins. Other items were: butter, separately accounted for by Mary Waters the dairymaid, £2 9s 6d; fruit, per Grimsdale the head gardener, £23 2s; for faggots and kindling wood £29. By far the largest of the receipts were payments by local farmers for the right to graze their cows and sheep in the Park, the animals being penned near the gate and taken in by the shepherd. These payments were called agistment, and in 1860 they amounted to £229.[13]

The twelfth Duke of Somerset died in 1883; he had five children, two sons and three daughters. One of the sons died as a result of a bite from a bear in India, and the other from TB or consumption. The youngest daughter, Lady Gwendolene, married Sir John William Ramsden, a Yorkshire landowner who built and owned most of Huddersfield. Lady Gwendolene was a very able woman and wrote about local history, especially the history of the Dukes of Somerset. During the First World War she established a military hospital at Bulstrode.

She and Sir William had a son called John Frecheville – a very enterprising man who took rubber plants from Kew and established the rubber industry in Malaya. He also invested in property in Kenya.[14]

The property in Kenya prospered. Cattle, sheep and fruit were farmed, but the main crop was sisal which was to be used for rope. In an effort to solve the problem of how to use the sisal after the removal of the fibre, a laboratory was set up in the stable block at Bulstrode, and it employed a good many local people. New laboratories were later built in the park where this work could be continued. The firm was called African Sisal Products.

In spite of his many enterprises, Sir John Frechville loved Bulstrode. He was an authority on rhododendrons and replanted the formal gardens which had originally been laid out by the first Earl of Portland, only the Long Water and the Round Pond being allowed to remain. The area near the house was laid out with symmetrical borders where fine roses were grown.[15] Beyond this, the ground became semi-wild and beautiful rhododendrons, azaleas and magnolias were planted among the older trees such as tall oaks, beech and especially cedars. Rarer species included sequoia and the handkerchief tree; bluebells grew among the trees and shrubs. In Sir John's time there were large greenhouses and a walled vegetable garden. Many of the men who lived round the common were employed in the house, gardens and park.

Sir John played polo on the camp, and was often in London. I was told that, when he was at Bulstrode, he liked to have a fresh fruit cake every day for tea. Lady Ramsden stayed at home, only going to London occasionally to attend the opera.

Sir John and Lady Ramsden had two sons; the elder was assassinated in Malaya in 1948, having served in the R.N.V.R. during World War II. The interest of William, the other, was drawn away from Bulstrode to the ancient estate of Muncaster near Ravenglass in Cumbria. The last Baron Muncaster, Josslyn Francis Pennington, who was childless, was a first cousin of Sir John and promised to make William Ramsden his heir on condition that he changed his name and fulfilled other conditions. Thereafter the family was known as Pennington-Ramsden, and lived at Muncaster where they still struggle to maintain the ancient castle and its beautiful gardens.

Sir William died in 1986 leaving a daughter, Phyllida, who married Patrick Gordon-Duff, and she has kindly given me the above information.

Some members of the Ramsden family lived in Camp House, near the crossing of the Oxford and Windsor Roads (now demolished), and Bulstrode House itself was unoccupied. During the Second World War it was used for a training centre, first for WAAFs and then for the RAF. After the war it passed through several hands. For a time the international organization called the Brüderhof established themselves there. This was a non-religious group who believed in a truly egalitarian society and whose members were forbidden to own any property, even a pair of shoes. They depended on charity for their necessities; for example, if a member needed shoes, say size 5, he or she would have to wait until these were donated. The members lived in family groups in different parts of the house. Suddenly, in the middle of the night, they received some sort of sign to leave. They got up and went, without even stopping to tidy their beds! They probably returned to South America, to their mother house.

After this Bulstrode was bought by the WEC (Worldwide Evangelization for Christ), an organization which provides living quarters for missionaries on their vacations from abroad and whose members are largely occupied in translating the scriptures into foreign, especially African, languages. This organization is very friendly to local churches and other organizations. People who want to visit the gardens are welcome, as long as they ask permission of the lady at the desk in the main hall.

In spite of the excellent work being done by WEC, it is difficult not to look back with nostalgia on the glamour shed on the neighbourhood by the distinguished families who occupied the ancient estate. From 1912 to 1935 my family lived in an old house by Latchmoor pond. It was exciting to be woken about 6 am by the sound of trotting horses as the string of polo ponies in charge of their grooms went by. I also remember Empire Day when all the local children, dressed in their best and wearing straw hats trimmed with pretty wreaths of buttercups and daisies, were invited to tea in the private gardens. As time passed, carriages were replaced by Rolls Royce cars, each with a rhinoceros horn on its bonnet. One of the worst days of my life was when our temperamental donkey, harnessed to a trap, lay down in the road and held up one of these lordly vehicles.

Notes

A History of Chalfont St. Peter & Gerrards Cross

I have not thought it necessary to repeat references given in Victoria County History of Bucks. (V.C.H.).

B   Bulstrode mss. (B.R.O.) (Ref. D/RA).
BAS   Bucks. Archaeological Society, County Museum, Aylesbury.
BRO   Bucks. Record Office, County Offices, Aylesbury.
(C)SPD   (Calendar of) State Papers, Domestic (PRO).
CSTP   Chalfont St. Peter.
DNB   *Dictionary of National Biography.*
GX   Gerrards Cross.
MR   Records of Manor of CSTP (BAS).
PCC   Will at Somerset House.
PRO   Public Record Office.
Records   *Records of Buckinghamshire.*

1. R. H. Lathbury: *History of Denham.* W.H. Ward and K.S. Block: *History of Iver.* R.E. Lloyd: *Church and Village of Fulmer.* H. Adams Clarke: 'Parish Church of Chalfont St. Giles'.
2. The 1876 6-in. O.S. map is useful. Tithe map of 1843 at Tithe Redemption Office, Worthing.
3. 1924 excavation of the Camp: Records xi, 283. Names: Mawer and Stenton, *Place-Names of Bucks.* Kilns: Records xiii, 252 and xiv, 153. Roman Roads: Viatores, *Roman Roads in S.E. Midlands* (1964).
4. Domesday entries: VCH i, 235, 270. Manorial history: VCH iii, 195, 280, 297. The Turvilles: B.H. Fowler, *Pipe-rolls of Bucks. and Beds.*
5. Records xvii, 20ff.
6. VCH I, 391: Bucks. Feet of Fines (Bucks. Record Society, Vol. IV): Berks., Bucks. and Oxon Archaeological Society, xi.
7. Feet of Fines, 9 EdII: Records xiv, 23: Inquisitions post mortem, 1300, 1342 and (Henry Drury) 1617 (PRO).
8. Mrs Elvey's invaluable article is based mainly upon an excellent collection of manorial records, belonging to the Rev. P.C. Moore, and deposited on loan with BAS. See also Missenden Cartulary (ed. J.G. Jenkins) especially ii, 174ff.
9. Before 1330 the king had granted these lands to the Abbess of Burnham, who complained that Geoffrey and others broke her house, the spindle and iron of her mill, and her hedges there, cut her corn, consumed her grass, carried away timber,

165

assaulted her steward, and so threatened her that for a long
time she could get no one to serve her. (Close Rolls, 1330).
Geoffrey was still fighting the case in 1346.

10. There is a useful sketch-map of the common fields in J.E.G.
    Bennel, *Notes towards a history of CSTP* (Typescript in local
    libraries).

11. PCC, Luffenham 31. On Chantry: VCH iii, 197. 'The chantry
    standeth in the churchyard' (Records xiii, 200) Mr Bennell tells
    me there are references in 1727-8 to a house in CSTP
    'formerly called the Chantry house'.

12. I.S. Leadem: *Domesday of Inclosures*, 190, 206.

12a. Records xviii, 73, 96.

13. VCH Herts, ii, 383. Patent roll, 7Ed VI, pt. 13.

14. See index refs. in VCH and CSPD.

15. BAS has a manuscript *Book of Bulstrode* by H.W. Bulstrode.
    There was a branch of the family at Beaconsfield; and it
    appears from PCC wills of Sir William (1527) and Maude
    (1531) that Sir William had a lease of Temple Bulstrode.

16. G. Redford and T.H. Riches, *History of Uxbridge* (1818), pp.
    205ff. PCC Mellershe 55.

17. *Notes and Queries*, 1863, pp. 150, 162.

18. A. Campling: *The Family of Drury*.

19. Records xvii, 189.

20. CSPD, 1601.

21. VCH iii, 280. BAS have several court-rolls and lists of tenants
    of Temple Bulstrode manor, which included lands at Tring,
    Ford, Stone, Wexham and Clewer.

22. MR35.

23. Samuel Aldridge's will, in 1652, refers to 'my house and lands
    in a common called Austen wood in CSTP, which I bought of
    Thomas Bulstrode Esq.' (PCC, Bower 154) On Mumfords and
    Ashwells, *Historic Monuments Commission*, i, 85.

24. Records, xv, 87.

25. CSPD 1577, cxv.

26. On the Manor of the Vicarage, see a characteristically careful
    article by Mr John Bennell, Records, xvii, 392.

27. Bucks. Sessions Records (1678–94), 422, 434: B 1/60:
    Records, xvii, 186.

28. Records, xvii, 416; xviii, 97.

29. F.C. Eeles: *Edwardian Inventories*, Bucks., p. 44.

30. MR, 28: Records, x, 408: PCC, Pynning, 41.

31. DNB: J. Foster, *Alumni Oxoniensis*.

32. Glebe terrier (Lincoln) and Tithe map. Some terriers are in
    BRO, some in Lincoln R.O.

33. CSPD: R.E. Lloyd, Fulmer: 1/223: Records, xv, 37 and xvii,
    208.

34. SPD, 16/336. Some records of this enquiry are printed in Records vi, 154, 245.
35. SPD, 287/31. Some of these interesting letters are printed in Records, vii, 97.
36. B 2/13. Pennington's purchase included Chalfont Lodge farm and the Swan inn.
37. On Pennington, see DNB: Mary Keeler, *The Long Parliament*: and especially Valerie Pearl, *London and the Outbreak of the Puritan Revolution*.
38. *Walker Revised*, ed. A. G. Matthews.
39. The House of Commons in September 1643 appointed John Chidwick; but Henry Gould's will, written in October 1644, and witnessed by both Chidwick and Holl, refers to 'my loving friend Thomas Holl, our minister in CSTP' (W.A. Shaw, *English Churches Under the Commonwealth*, ii, 295: will in BRO). Thomas Holl B.A. was ordained priest by the Bishop of Oxford in 1614, and had been for some years vicar of Cholesbury, Co. Bucks. (Lincoln, L.C. 5, 132 and Registers).
40. CSPD and Civil War Tracts.
41. *Survey of Livings*, 1650 (PRO, c. 94): W.A. Shaw, op. cit.: Mr E.J. Briden kindly transcribed and sent the entry from Chesham Parish Church register.
42. On the early Quakers here, see Ellwood's autobiography: Bucks. Record Society, volumes I and VII: W.H. Summers, *Jordans and the Chalfonts*. On Milton's acquaintance with the Bulstrodes, Penningtons and Ellwood, see Masson's *Life of Milton*.
43. T. Butterfield. PCC, 1655/291: Wetherly (1641), Monk (1649), Cawdrey (1639), Good (1647), all at BRO.
44. On Mumfords, note 23 above. The Whitchurch wills illustrate the progress of the family, and of the house: Richard, 1647 (BRO): Thomas, 1691 (PCC, Fane 159): Richard, 1709 (PCC), Young 224). On the Church House affair, Chancery Petty Bag, Charity Inquisitions 28/23 (PRO).
45. Glebe terrier, 1724 (Lincoln).
46. St. John's College Muniments, xli, 1 to 17.
47. CSPD 1666–76: Treasury Book 1669 et seq. Fulmer deeds. BRO: CSTP register.
48. B 2/20, 2/25. On Trevor, DNB and Le Neve's 'Knights': register baptism.
49. Articles by H.M. Balfour in *Law Journal*, 1929. G.W. Keeton in *Lord Chancellor Jeffreys and the Stuart Cause* points out that it is difficult to penetrate to facts about Jeffreys, and that Macaulay's well-known pen-portrait is based upon heavily-biased Whig sources.
50. 2nd Ledger Book of Chipping Wycombe, 1685. Macaulay's *History of England*, c. iv.

51. Alex. Smith: *Lives of the ... Highwaymen* (ed. 1926), p. 41. See also pp. 140ff.
52. B 1/44.
53. H.M. Hyde, *Judge Jeffreys*. There are elevations and a plan on Fisher's map.
54. PCC 1690/130. But see note 49 above, and Luttrell's Diary.
55. B 1/60. On Bentinck, M.S. Grew, *William Bentinck and William III*.
56. B 1/66. Jeffreys in 1686 had been given leave to divert Hedgerley Lane (CSPD, May 12).
57. Camden's *Britannia* (1720); Speculum CSTP (Lincoln RO). When Portland sold to Somerset in 1811, the deed refers to Schoolhouse field and John Appleton, school-master. Schoolhouse field, in Bull Lane, was part of 'Raylands Mead' estate. (Information from the late Mr E.G. Eardley Wilmot, and B 1/108).
58. Hedgerley parish register. Historic Manuscripts Commission, Portland, iv, 504.
59. On the architectural history of Bulstrode, see a valuable article by John Harris in *Architectural Review*, November 1968, also W.H. Wadham Powell in *Home Counties Magazine*, vol. IX (1907–8).
60. Records, xi, 60. The church was well restored in 1966.
61. Ward and Block's *Iver*.
62. CSTP ratebook (Parish chest): Burke's Commoners, s.v. W. Palmer: BRO deeds, CSTP and Fulmer: PCC, Browne 237, Lisle 30: Treasury Book 1715: Foster, Oxford Alumni. Mr Wilkins was dilatory in paying his local rates: 'Spent at ye Packhorse when Mr Wilkins was strained, 3s.' (Overseers' Accounts, 1740).
63. Neither is to be confused with Charles Churchill (1734–64), son of an Essex clergyman, poet and member of the Hellfire Club. Mr L.M. Wulcko kindly communicated the substance of three Private Acts relating to this settlement: 23 Geo. II, c. 18; 9 Geo. III, c. 53; 32 Geo. III, c. 39. The property bought from Lister Selman Esq. in 1755 included, besides Chalfont Place or the Old House, another house on the S.E. side of it, a farmhouse, and a limekiln: but the other house, farmhouse and limekiln had been demolished before the property was sold in 1794. Oakgrove Farm and 71 acres Lister Selman had bought from Robert Hill, blacksmith.
64. *Walpole's Letters*. (ed. Toynbee) July 5, 1755.
65. Quoted in brochure of Chalfont Park Hotel (1921): N. Pevsner, *Buckinghamshire*. Walpole, July 4, 1760.
66. Walpole: May 7, 1755; Jan 26, 1762; Oct. 3, 1763. The Duchess was the granddaughter of the Duke of Newcastle, from whom she inherited a large estate, including Welbeck, Co.

Notts; and after her husband died in 1768, her son, the 3rd Duke of Portland, lived at Welbeck whilst she remained at Bulstrode. *Mrs Delany's Letters* (ed. Lady Llanover) (1861–62). *Mrs Montague's Letters* (1809–13).

67. Delaney, Sept. 3, 1769.
68. DNB: information from Mr C.F. Le Mesurier. Mrs Lybbe Powys, Diary, 13.7.1769.
69. Delany, July 1779.
70. Delany, August 1778.
71. Delany, Nov. 1781: VCH, ii, 223ff, 228.
72. Information from the Queen's Librarian and Mr L.M. Wulcko: *Gentleman's Magazine*, 1809, 1813. Gott died in 1809. His daughter Sarah married her cousin, Sir Harford Jones.
73. E.S. Roscoe, *Penn's Country*, revd. enl. ed. London: Longmans Green, 1914, pp. 103–04.
74. Delany, August 1776: DNB: E.S. Roscoe, *Penn's Country*, p. 39. The 3rd Duke (1738–1809) married a daughter of William, 4th Duke of Devonshire.
75. H. Repton: *Landscape Gardening* (1840), p. 141. The Duke 'gave leave to all persons to pass through the park, and even encouraged the neighbouring inhabitants to play cricket on the lawn' (p. 602).
76. John Harris, op. cit. Georgiana, Duchess of Devonshire, wrote in 1787 of her agent, Mr Heaton: 'He has just finished the extricating of the Duke of Portland from distress, and even by useful speculation gives him the prospect of affluence' (Bessborough; *Georgiana, Duchess of Devonshire*).
77. Names from Register, Sessions Records, MR, *passim*. On Overseers Accounts: Records XVIII, 3ff.
78. MR, and information from Mr Wulcko.
79. Brasenose College archives, Iver. The Woodhill estate (200 acres) was sold by Henry Bulstrode to Sir Sampson Darrell in 1630. There is a sketch-map, drawn by the College Bursar in 1680. In 1778 the house was leased to Mrs Elizabeth Hutchins. Way mss. (BRO) 57/5, 57/9 are Notices of Sale.
80. VCH, iii, 196: MR 17–20.
81. Glebe terriers, 170d, 1707: Speculum, CSTP, 1705–23 (Lincoln).
82. Bishops' Register (PRO), Foster, *Oxford Alumni*: M.J. Simmonds, 'Merchant Taylor Fellows of St. John's: information from the President of St. John's College'. A.H. Cocks: *Church Bells of Bucks.*, p. 339.
83. The rampant lion was part of the Trevor crest. William Courtney and his brother Robert had other farms in CSP, and also the Red Lion alehouse (Poor Rate book).
84. W.H. Summers, *Congregational Churches in S. Bucks.* etc.: Urwick, *Nonconformity in Herts.*

85. Poor Law Union Papers (M.H. 12), vol. 380.
86. Thomas Hibbert, who bought the Chalfont Park estate from Churchill's trustees, was succeeded in 1819 by his brother Robert. Both had been merchants in Jamaica, where Robert married Letitia Nembhard. Robert's first cousin, another Robert, was founder of the Hibbert Trust (DNB and information from Mr L. Wulcko).
87. Sale catalogue, British Museum Map Room.
88. E.A. and W. Seymour, *Correspondence of Two Brothers*, August 1811. June 1813: 'I hope you have run down to Bulstrode to enjoy its delightful shades. I could wish myself in the lime walk with you.' Amongst Bulstrode papers, BRO, is a sketch-plan of what remained of the house in 1817. Leases: B 2/363, 365. There are particulars prepared for a sale in 1814 in a rent-book kindly lent by Mr J. Hetherington.
89. H. Janes, *The Red Barrel*: F.C. Cass, *East Barnet*: Annual Register, 1852. *Windsor and Eton Express*, May 15th, 1852.
90. B/4/138.
91. The ladies asked again for a piece of land on the opposite side of the Oxford road, for a sexton's house, 'almost a necessary appendage under the isolated, though valuable, position of the Church', but later withdrew this request, B 4/138, 143.
92. John Bramley-Moore (1800–1886), chairman of Liverpool Docks, had been a notable figure in Brazil (DNB). W.J. Bramley Moore's many books included in 1912, a life of his cousin Theodore Pennell, Missionary in N.W. India (Venn, Alum. Cantab: B.M. Library Catalogue). Hardy & Sons demolished Bulstrode in 1860, and a new house, designed by Benjamin Ferrey, was built (B 5: Pevsner, Bucks.).
93. Parish Chest: National Society Records; Mr J. Bennell.
94. Redford and Riches, *Uxbridge*, 105. Ogilby's Road-maps: 1853 Directory: O.S. maps.
95. Presumably the Oakgrove farm land (see above p. 48), which was occupied 1790–1800 by Francis Peter Mallett Esq., Sheriff of Bucks. in 1793, described in *Gentleman's Magazine*, November 1799, as 'a very respectable person', who had been 'an eminent cabinet maker in Clerkenwell'.
96. Army List, 1840.
97. See E. Mayne Reid, *Captain Mayne Reid*, (1900).
98. Information from Alderman E.L. Colston and other residents.
99. From the first Minute Book of GX Parish Council, by permission.
100. In 1968 the headmaster was Mr P.E. Rowlett. A new Infants School was built in Lovel End.

The History of Bulstrode

Throughout these notes the references to the Rev. G.C. Edmonds *History of Chalfont St. Peter and Gerrards Cross*, in the first half of this volume are cited as 'Edmonds'.

1. Early Times

1. B. Stainton, *The Archaeology of the Chilterns*, ed. K. Branigan (Chess Valley Archaeological Society, 1994), p.12; J.F. Head, *Early Man in South Buckinghamshire* (Bristol, 1953).
2. L. Barfield, 'Excavation of a Mesolithic site at Gerrards Cross'. *Records of Bucks.*, 20 (III), 1977, pp. 302-336; Stainton, *op. cit.*, p. 28.
3. Stainton, *op. cit.*, p. 31; also Head, *op. cit.*
4. Edmonds, p. 7.
5. Stainton, *op. cit.*, p. 58.
6. K. Branigan, *Latimer – Belgic and Roman* (Bristol, EVAHS, 1971).
7. Stainton, *op. cit.*, p. 127.
8. A. Mawer and F.M. Stenton, *Place Names of Buckinghamshire* (Cambridge Univ. Press, 2nd edn, 1969).
9. J.E.A. Jollipe, *Constitutional History of Mediaeval England* (London, 1937), p. 140.
10. *The Anglo-Saxon Chronicle*, ed. J. Ingram (Everyman Library, 1917), p. 163.
11. *Victoria County History*, Vol. I (1969), pp. 232, 222; G. Lipscomb, *History and Antiquities of Buckinghamshire*, Part VIII (1847), p. 571; this manor was clearly on the river.
12. K.A. Bailey, 'The Manor in Doomsday Buckinghamshire. I'. *Records of Bucks*, 38, 1995-6, p. 133.
13. Edmonds, pp. 14, 27-28; H.W. Bulstrode, *The Book of Bulstrode*, p. 9 (MS copy in the library of the Bucks. Archaeological Society in Aylesbury).

2. The Bulstrode Family and the Brasses in Upton Church

1. H.W. Bulstrode, *The Book of Bulstrode*, pp. 8, 10, 11.
2. Edmonds, p. 7.
3. Bulstrode, *op. cit.*, p. 12.
4. *Ibid.*, p.14.
5. *Ibid.*, p.13.

171

6. Edmonds, p. 8; E. Briden, *The Parish Church of Chalfont St. Peter*, 1979, p. 2.
7. E.M. Elvey, 'The Abbot of Missenden's estates in Chalfont St. Peter', *Records of Bucks*, 17, 1965, p. 26. Robert de Montford was a tenant of the Abbey in 1333.
8. Edmonds, p. 10.
9. I. Wilson, *The Turin Shroud* (Penguin, 1978), pp. 202-10.
10. Bulstrode, *op. cit.*, pp. 19-20; Edmonds, pp. 9-10, 166n13.
11. C. le Mesurier, article in M. Rice (ed.), *A South Bucks Village*, p. 30.
12. J. Bennell, 'The manor of the vicarage of Chalfont St. Peter', *Records of Bucks*, 17(5), 1965, p. 392.
13. Bulstrode, *op. cit.*, pp. 19, 23.
14. *Ibid.*, p. 23.
15. *Ibid.*
16. *Ibid.*, p. 22.
17. A.M. Baker, 'Upton church and the Bulstrode brasses', *Records of Bucks* (in press).
18. 'The old church at Upton', *Records of Bucks*, 1 (1854-5), 201; also *Proceedings of the Society*, 7 (1891-2), p. 28.
19. G. Lipscomb, *The History and Antiquities of Buckinghamshire* (London, 1847), Part 8, p. 575.
20. N. Pevsner, *Buildings of England. Buckinghamshire*, 1994, p. 624.
21. *Records of Bucks*, p. 1.
22. Royal Commission for Historical Monuments (1912), p. 278.
23. Maxwell Fraser, *History of Slough* (1886); an excellent account of the raising of funds is given by Mrs S. Neal, *Go Beastly Bomb, Why Fall on Slough?* (1998).
24. Royal Commission for Historical Monuments (1912), p. 278.
25. Wilson, *op.cit.*, pp. 202–10.
26. W.G. Lack, H.M. Stuchfield and P.J. Whittemore, *The Monumental Brasses of Buckinghamshire* (1994), p. 221. I am very grateful to Mr Lack for sending me photocopies of notes made by Canon Rutter from notes by Browne Willis (Oxford, Bodleian Lib. MS. Browne Willis), and also for allowing me to reproduce plates of the brasses from his book.
27. *Records of Bucks*, 7 (1891-2), p. 28.
28. The Institute had not yet received its royal charter.
29. Lack *et al.*, *op. cit.*, p. 223.
30. Lipscomb, *op. cit.*, Part 8, p. 574.
31. *Ibid.*, p. 575; Lack *et al.*, *op. cit.*, p. 224.
32. Lipscomb, *op. cit.*, Part 1, p. 28.
33. Lipscomb, *op. cit.*, Part 8, p. 575.
34. Lack *et al.*, *op. cit.*, p. 224.
35. Edmonds, p. 29.
36. *Ibid.*, plate opposite p. 48. For a general background of archi-

tecture and the arts in the early seventeenth century, see Roy Strong, *Henry Prince of Wales and England's Lost Renaissance* (London, 1986).

37. C.V. Wedgewood, *The Great Rebellion*, Vol. II, p. 143. The Royalist army was beseiged by the Parliamentarians in Reading. The garrison was eventually surrounded, but they and other Royalist soldiers foraged in the Vale of Aylesbury. Henry defended Aylesbury, but he was now getting old and died in this same year. (Edmonds, p. 37).

38. Lack *et al.*, *op. cit.*, p. 222.

39. Lipscomb, *op. cit.*, Part 8, p. 575.

40. G.M. Trevelyan, *England Under the Stuarts* (London, Methuen, 1938), pp. 225 *et seq.*

41. M. Rice (ed.) *A South Bucks Village* (1980), p. 32.

42. Wedgewood, *op. cit.*, Vol. II, p. 144.

43. 'State of parish churches', *Records of Bucks*, 6 (1887-91), p. 166.

3. **The Houses**

1. H.W. Bulstrode, *The Book of Bulstrode*, p. 12 (MS copy in the library of the Bucks. Archaeological Society in Aylesbury).

2. *Ibid.*, p. 21.

3. M. Carton and J. Hatherley, 'Mediaeval Parks of Bucks', *Records of Bucks*, XX, pp. 431-440; their brasses are in Upton church (see above, Chapter II).

4. Reproduced on p. 115; also J. Harris, 'Bulstrode', *Architectural Review*, 124 (No. 742), Nov. 1968. I am indebted to Mr Harris for giving me much information and for sending me plans of the house, and allowing me to reproduce illustrations from his article.

5. Report by Archbishop Laud, quoted by Edmonds, p. 35.

6. *The Autobiography and Correspondence of Mary Granville, Mrs Delany*, 6 vols, ed. Lady Llandover (R. Bentley, London, 1861-2), Series 2, Vol. 3, p. 175; E.F. Anson, *Mary Hamilton aft. Mrs J.D. Dickenson at Court and at Home from Letters and Diaries, 1756-1816*, p. 143.

7. Edmonds, p. 42-43.

8. *Ibid.*, p. 44.

9. G. Paston, *Mrs Delany, a Memoir* (London, Grant Richards, 1900), p. 224.

10. Edmonds, p. 61, quoting Walpole's correspondence.

11. Official Report, *Records of Bucks*, 30 (1988); also M. Rice, *op. cit.*, p. 8.

12. Extract from the Way papers in Bucks Record Office, Aylesbury

(Bucks County Record Office D/W. 1/22. 183; the Way family succeeded the Hills at Moat Farm. (Communicated by the late Colin Le Mesurier).

4. Bulstrode in the Eighteenth Century

1. Schazmann (translated by Cox), *The History of a European Family*.
2. M.S. Grew, *William Bentinck and William III*; Edmonds, p. 45; J. Harris, 'Bulstrode', *Architectural Review*, 124 (No. 742), 1958. I am indebted to Mr John Harris for much information.
3. This is the second engraving by Bowles. There is a large framed copy hanging in the entrance to Bulstrode House; it is reproduced by S. Festing, 'Rare flowers and fantastic breeds', *Country Life*, 12 June 1986, p. 1655.
4. Edmonds, p. 45.
5. Edmonds, pp. 45, 168n59.
6. Harris, *op. cit.*, p. 319.
7. *Guide to the Church of St. Andrew in the Wardrobe*, nd.
8. The Vertue MS., *Walpole Society Annual*, Vol. II, p. 30, and Vol. IV, pp. 47-89, 139.
9. A.S. Tuberville, *Welbeck Abbey and its Owners* (1938), Vol. I, pp. 334 *et seq.*; *Works of Dean Swift*, Vol. XVIII, pp. 199-200.
10. Tuberville, *op. cit.*, Vol. I, pp. 340 *et seq.*; facing p. 320 there is a portrait of Henrietta by Kneller.
11. *Ibid.*, p. 332.
12. G. Paston, *Mrs Delany, a Memoir* (Grant Richards, London, 1900), pp. 123, 192.
13. Tuberville, *op. cit.*, Vol. I, facing p. 332; M. Webb, *M. Rysbrack* (1954).
14. Tuberville, *op. cit.*, Vol. II, p. 20 and note.
15. Paston, *op. cit.*, p. 105.
16. Communicated to me by J. Bennell Esq. (probably from the archives of the Royal Commission on Historical MS; it cannot now be traced either there or at Nottingham University where the Portland papers are deposited).
17. A. Foreman, *Georgina, Duchess of Devonshire* (Flamingo Press, 1998-9), p. 20.
18. E.J. Climenson, *Elizabeth Montague, Queen of the Blue Stockings. Correspondence*, Vol. I (1906), p. 49.
19. *Autobiography and Correspondence* ... (full reference below), Series, Vol. III, p. 175. Much interesting information about life at Bulstrode can be gleaned from the many books about Mrs Delany; the most important source is *The Autobiography and Correspondence of Mary Granville, Mrs Delany*, 6 vols, ed. Lady

Llandover (R. Bentley, London, 1861-2). Also, Paston, *op. cit.*; C.E. Vulliamy, *Aspasia: A Contemporary Eulogy* (London, Geoffrey Bles, 1925); R. Hayden, *Mrs Delany, Her Life and Her Flowers* (London, Colonnade (British Library), 1980).

There are two interesting and well illustrated articles by S. Festing in *Country Life*, 1986: 'Pt. I. Rare flowers and fantastic breeds', June 12, p. 1684 *et seq.*, 'Pt. II. Grace without triviality', June 19, p. 1772, *et seq.*; unfortunately the author does not give references or a bibliography.

20. Paston, *op. cit.*, p. 102.
21. *Ibid.*, p. 106.
22. Climenson, *op. cit.*, Vol. I, p. 23.
23. Paston, *op. cit.*, p. 107.
24. Tuberville, *op. cit.*, Vol. I, pp. 351-2; J. Nichols, *Literary Anecdotes of the Eighteenth Century*, Vol. IV, pp. 112-46; Ballard, *Learned Ladies: A Galaxy of Governesses*.
25. Delany, *Autobiography, op. cit.*, Vol. III, pp. 321-3.
26. Tuberville, *op. cit.*, Vol. I, p. 22.
27. Hayden, *op. cit.*, p. 92.
28. Paston, *op. cit.*, p. 106.
29. *Ibid.*, p. 193.
30. *Ibid.*, p. 137.
31. *Dictionary of National Biography* (Lightfoot); *Proceedings of the Linnaean Society* (1890); Edmonds, p. 62; Festing, *op. cit.*, Pt. II, p. 1773.
32. Delany, *Autobiography, op. cit.*, Vol. I, p. 445, and Vol. II, p. 253.
33. P. Dance, *Shell Collecting* (Faber & Faber, 1966); Festing, *op. cit.*, p. 1774 reproduces beautiful drawings of shells said to be by the Duchess. She is believed to have established the first systematic identification of shells.
34. Festing, *op. cit.*, Pt. II, p. 1773, with illustration; Paston, *op. cit.*, p. 189.
35. Edmonds, pp. 61-63.
36. *Diary* (Lybbe Powys), quoted by Edmonds, pp. 62, 169n68.
37. Joseph D. Hooker (ed.), *Journal of the Right Hon. Sir Joseph Banks* (London, Macmillan, 1896); C. Lyle, *Sir Joseph Banks*, p. 180; J.R. Muir, *The Life and Achievements of Captain James Cook* (Blackie, London, 1939), pp. 130, 152, etc.
38. Delany, *Autobiography, op. cit.*, Vol. II, p. 383.
39. A.P. Paterson, *The Chelsea Physic Garden* (London Parochial Charities).
40. Paston, *op. cit.*, pp. 218, 230; the subject is discussed in the book by Hayden, *op. cit.*, with beautiful illustrations.
41. Delany, *Autobiography, op. cit.*, Vol. 3, pp. 460, 477, etc.; Tuberville, *op. cit.*, p. 1; Hayden, *op. cit.*, p. 128; E.F. Anson, *Mary Hamilton aft. Mrs J. D. Dickenson at Court and at Home*

from Letters and Diaries 1756-1816, Vol. 2, pp. 175, 177.

42. Collected Walpole correspondence, Vol. IV, p. 139; Vertue, *Walpole Society Annual,* Vol. IV, pp. 68-70, 147, Vol. V, pp. 28, 68, 140 (Vertue used to travel round England to record works of art, taking a retinue of ten servants and six coach horses).

43. Walpole, Diary, Dec. 27, 1775.

44. See above p. 146; also Festing, *op. cit.,* Pt. I, p. 1686.

45. Paston, *op. cit.,* p. 224.

46. *Ibid.,* p. 226.

47. *Ibid.,* p. 236; Edmonds, p. 63.

48. Dickenson, *op. cit.,* Vol. 2, p. 257; for a charming silhouette of the old ladies at their work, see Hayden, *op. cit.,* p. 165.

49. Festing, *op. cit.,* Pt. I, p. 1685, includes a reproduction of the engraving on the cover of the catalogue, of which there is a copy in the British Library.

5. **Bulstrode in the Nineteenth and Twentieth Centuries**

1. For the tremendous power wielded by the Cavendish family in the eighteenth century, see A. Foreman, *Georgina, Duchess of Devonshire* (Flamingo Press, 1998-9); this book gives a very detailed account of the politics of this period.

2. A.S. Tuberville, *Welbeck Abbey and its Owners* (1938), Vol. II, p. 60.

3. *Ibid.,* pp. 82, 136.

4. J. Harris, 'Bulstrode', *Architectural Review,* 124 (No. 742), 1958; this article includes pictures of all three plans. I am deeply indebted to Mr Harris for information and for sending me the plans.

5. H. Repton, *Landscape Gardening* (1840), p. 141. Repton compiled 'Red Books' for each estate on which he worked; there is a copy of the Bulstrode Red Book in the Library of the Victoria and Albert Museum.

6. Harris, *op. cit.;* Edmonds, pp. 71, 170n88.

7. *Dictionary of National Biography.*

8. Edmonds, p. 71.

9. Estate papers deposited in Archive Office, Aylesbury.

10. Harris, *op. cit.,* p. 125.

11. Estate papers deposited in Archive Office, Aylesbury.

12. Edmonds, p. 72; E.C. Rouse and Rev. G. Harrison, *Gerrards Cross and its Parish Church* (1969).

13. Estate papers deposited in Archive Office, Aylesbury.

14. The information in this part was given to the author by Lady Phyllida Gordon-Duff Pennington.

15. *The Gardener's Magazine,* 7 March, 1914.

Index

References to captions on illustrations pages are indicated by numerals in **bold** type.

183